Additional Praise for
She's Unlikeable

"I was already in awe of Aparna's resilience after watching her journey unfold on and off the show, but her memoir gives me more of a reason to look up to her. Her sharp memory transports me to her hometown in Houston; the way she describes her travels makes me want to catch a flight; the wisdom she aptly shares and the witty comebacks she writes will have you believing anything in life is possible. There's nothing she can't achieve, and she will make you feel the same about your journey, giving the reader a clear purpose as she details her ups and downs beautifully. With more life for her to live, I am impatiently waiting for the second memoir."
—**Trisha Sakhuja-Walia**, CEO and cofounder of BrownGirlMagazine.com

"A true reading pleasure, *She's Unlikeable* connects the dots for those striving toward a more authentic existence through Aparna's recounting of her life lessons. This book is perfect for anyone tapping into their own need to live a life outside of set societal milestones—a life full of surprises, immense joy, and exploration of self."
—**Natalie Franke**, author of *Built to Belong*

"Pointed, often humorous, and at times refreshingly surprising, *She's Unlikeable* invites us to sit down with the Aparna we missed out on in *Indian Matchmaking*—an intelligent, witty, and unabashedly honest woman who tells her tales of resilience in the most disarming way on every page."
—**Jessica Batten**, TV personality

"An important read for those who are ready to break free of living life on other people's terms. Who are ready to chart their own course. Who won't let other's criticisms, perceived or real, hold them back. Who want to live more fully. (And who also love a little behind-the-scenes of reality television.)"

—**Darrah Brustein**, hybrid life coach and business strategist

"*She's Unlikeable* should have been titled *She's Relatable.* The book gave me goosebumps as I absorbed all the pages over a weekend read that wouldn't let me put this book down. Aparna reflects the many stages of not just an Indian woman but all women. I loved the genuine vulnerability and sharing of challenging moments when she felt deflated and beat, which remind us that even in those experiences, we should learn from and ultimately champion and cheerlead each other. This book, just like the author, is authentic and relatable."

—**Sonya Singh**, author of *Sari, Not Sari*

She's Unlikeable

She's Unlikeable

And Other Lies That Bring Women Down

APARNA SHEWAKRAMANI

CHICAGO
REVIEW
PRESS

Published by Chicago Review Press Incorporated
814 North Franklin Street
Chicago, Illinois 60610
ISBN 978-1-64160-666-0

Library of Congress Control Number: 2021949107

Typesetting: Nord Compo

Printed in the United States of America
5 4 3 2 1

Thank you to my beloved mama,
who gave me the greatest gift of all: she believed in me.

And thank you to all the immigrant mothers who held
their daughters' dreams in their hearts, whether they
understood the magnitude of the fruition of those
dreams or not. We owe our ultimate heights to you.

CONTENTS

AUTHOR'S NOTE

THIS BOOK is not about my participation on *Indian Matchmaking*, though it does, of course, include my time on the show. Several viewers and critics of the Netflix series have referred to me as a "polarizing figure." And I can see why. For me, *Indian Matchmaking* was a life-altering experience. It was filled with ups and downs. It had surprises both good and bad. It was at once heartbreaking and heart-mending. And throughout it all, one thing stands out: the show has been a source of *good* in my life. It was a remarkably positive experience, one of which I am proud, one that I would repeat a thousand times over. To the entire team at the show: I hope you know that my heart is filled with appreciation and gratitude for every single one of you. *Thank you.*

ACKNOWLEDGMENTS

A SIMPLE THANK-YOU will never be enough for those who have stood by me through this book's journey, but I will try to share my endless gratitude here.

First and foremost, my dearest agent, CeCe Lyra. You are the most empathetic, generous, intelligent cheerleader of all I have to say on paper and also all I have to say behind the scenes. Thank you for empowering me when I was at my lowest. Thank you for lifting me higher when I was already soaring. We're in this together, always.

My editor, Kara Rota. You truly believed this was a story worth telling. You brought these "rules to living life" *to* life and worked tirelessly to coordinate the masterminds behind the title "She's Unlikeable." You gave this book its name and its identity.

The Chicago Review Press team. I am forever grateful for your creativity, unparalleled logistics, and never-ending flexibility in elevating this book to its best state, including Cynthia Sherry as publisher; Michelle Williams and Devon Freeny on editorial; Sadie Teper, leading cover design; Jen DePoorter on marketing; Hailey Peterson and Alisse Goldsmith-Wissman heading up publicity; Allison Felus in production; and Alayna Parsons-Valles as the administrative lead.

To my family—my sister, Vansa, for unconditional love and never-ending "big sister" protection; my brother-in-law, Darrin, for supporting us all without question and without limit; and though she's received the entire dedication of this book, my mother for being my ever-present model of resilience, grit, and grace.

To all my friends, and especially to those who showed up in every unexpected, beautiful way after the launch of *Indian Matchmaking*. Your strength, reassurance, solidarity, and love sustained me. A special thank you to Divya, Muneezeh, and Smita. You three lifted me up when I couldn't stand myself. You are my team. You are also my sisters.

To my fans from *Indian Matchmaking*. Your voices were loud and clear when you stood up for me and for women everywhere who deserve a voice not only in matchmaking but in every space they occupy. Thank you for joining #TeamAparna and for continuing to dismantle the archaic systems steeped with misogynistic tropes dictating the likeability of women. We, as a society, are better than those stereotypes, and I am forever grateful to each one of you for embodying these ideals.

To the media outlets and journalists who amplified my voice in ways I could have never accomplished myself. A heartfelt thank-you for magnifying my words around the world and sharing my story through your own insights into reality television and feminism today.

To the whole cast of *Indian Matchmaking*. My story is merely one of many when it comes to this show about our collective search for love. I am lucky to call each one of you my friend. A special word of gratitude to Shekar, who started as a date and ended as a true friend. Your support when I was at my lowest, my most panicked, and my most defeated will never be forgotten. Also to Ankita, you are family. I trust you with my biggest dreams and my tiniest fears.

To Smriti Mundhra. You call me "sis" but also embody that with your kindness, protection, and deep desire to see me shine. I, for one, cannot wait to see the awareness and justice you will bring to this world through your intelligence, creativity, and empathy.

And to everyone who ever hated, despised, or detested me due to my portrayal on a television show. Thank you. You are the very reason I continue to speak up for ambitious, driven women who want love but aren't willing to settle for anything less than the partner they believe they deserve. You are the reason I live my truth every single day.

1

FIND YOUR OWN LIFEBOAT
AND HANG ON

I'M AT THE LAX AIRPORT, about to flag down a lifeboat. I don't know this yet.

For now, I am moving slowly through the boarding line with fellow group 2 passengers snaking around the coffee kiosk planted in the middle of the terminal's thoroughfare. My eyes are heavy. My tote bag bites into my shoulder. I am aching to sit in my plane seat and be taken back home to Houston, where a mountain of litigation briefs awaits me. Most of all, I am feeling defeated. I don't want to be in this city anymore.

Why am I still in Los Angeles? For a first date—a *failed* first date.

I came to L.A. to visit a friend. I stayed an extra day to meet a guy. We'll call him Mr. Gentle-but-Rambling Giant. Mr. Gentle-but-Rambling Giant and I met on a South Asian–focused dating app called Dil Mil, which loosely translates to "when hearts meet." As far as dating apps go, it's not an awful name. The date, however, was just that. Which is unfortunate because I had high hopes for Mr. Gentle-but-Rambling Giant, a tall entrepreneur with a charming smile.

The entire date lasted eleven hours, its longevity the result of both logistics and persistency. I really wanted to make this one work. Feeling hopeless about the South Asian dating scene in Houston—a repetitive stream of the same ten to fifteen men I've already dined with or swiped *no* on—I knew I had to expand my small pond into the ocean. For me, that meant slotting in dates when I traveled. Mr. Gentle-but-Rambling Giant and I met for coffee at 4:00 PM at a Beverly Hills café and moved to a luxe wine bar around 10:00 PM. Enough time for me to learn that Mr. Gentle-but-Rambling Giant is preternaturally attached to his suburban Orange County lifestyle and that we shared zero chemistry.

I would've cut the date short if I hadn't kept convincing myself that maybe, just maybe, if I stayed a little longer, I would like him more. Something would magically click at hour five . . . or seven . . . or ten. Except it didn't. And when I finally admitted defeat, I realized that my friend had failed to provide me with a fob to get into her building, which meant that Mr. Gentle-but-Rambling Giant and I had to wait in his car outside her complex for someone to let me in. The tableau we were stuck in was an unhappy one: Mr. Gentle-but-Rambling Giant was pattering on about his Santa Barbara wine getaways while I yawned and eyed the front gate. I felt stranded. And bored. And absolutely eager to run away. All at once.

Finally, at 3:00 AM, a late-night partygoer stumbled out of an Uber, at which point I hastily said goodbye to Mr. Gentle-but-Rambling Giant and followed the partygoer inside. Shockingly, Mr. Gentle-but-Rambling Giant seemed surprised by my eagerness to catch the slowly closing gate. I had no regrets about leaving him behind. He was not for me. Of this, I was sure. Still, I was proud for putting myself out there. Proud but, like I said, defeated. I had hoped against hope that this guy would be different.

What is it about defeat that makes us want to go home?

My flight wasn't scheduled until 6:00 PM, but in that moment, as I climbed into bed with a full face of makeup and tears of exhaustion in the corners of my eyes, I knew I had to get out of Los Angeles as quickly as possible. I was alone in my friend's home—she'd gone to Las Vegas for a birthday party. Her multi-story, split-level apartment somehow felt both empty and cramped. I thumbed my way to the United Airlines app. I knew what to do.

Within minutes, I was on the phone with a representative from the airline premier status line. I allowed myself to find my "sad" voice—not a challenging task when you're experiencing the failure of an extended first date. Not that I shared that part. Of course not. Instead, I explained that my dog was ill. *Sniff.* Could she please help me get back to Houston and with no change fees or additional cost?

It worked: in a matter of minutes, I was booked on the next available direct flight, all penalties waived. (Pro tip: the sick-dog excuse always works. All's fair in homesickness and dating—and this was both.) A small comfort. I set my phone on the nightstand and fell into a listless sleep. I had an 11:00 AM flight to catch.

A few hours later, my alarm went off.

As I threw my clothes into my trusty purple carry-on suit-case, I couldn't help but wonder: How many more of these dating attempts—big or small, on a plane or at a local wine bar—would I have to endure before I found Mr. Right? It's all I could think of as I headed to the airport.

That's how I got here. *Here* being the line to board the airplane. About to signal a lifeboat. Again, not that I know that. Not yet.

Boarding lines are a socially acceptable form of torture. They're messy and interminably lengthy, not to mention inefficient and slow. Not a great thing when you're already feeling crushed by your nonexistent love life. Which is why I pull out my phone.

Mindless Facebook scrolling is all I have right now. It'll distract me from the wait, if not from my heavy heart.

I am shifting from hip to hip when I spot a friend's post with three questions. I read each one, answers firing in my head in rapid succession.

"Are you single?" *Yes.*

"Are you South Asian?" *Yes.*

"Do you want to get married?" *Yes!*

The next line is a call to action.

"Then send an inquiry to xyz email address."

I look up from my phone. The gate still hasn't been opened. Ahead of me, group 1 is still impatiently waiting. I read the questions one more time.

Can you blame me for thinking it was a sign? For deeming it kismet?

If you can, you are not single, South Asian, and hoping to get married.

I click on the email address and quickly draft a note expressing my interest in participating in the docuseries and inquiring about next steps. I board the flight and turn off my phone.

By the time I land in Houston, the response is in my inbox.

As we're taxiing to the gate, I reply to the email requesting a thirty-minute Skype call with an attached application. I promise the completed forms before our call, which is quickly set up for the next day at 3:00 PM. It will be tricky, video chatting from my rigid workplace, but I will just have to shut my door and hope I'm not interrupted. I reply to each question on the forms promptly—I want them to be impressed by my responsiveness. In proper Aparna rationale, I figure no one would want to cast someone who didn't provide information in a timely manner. In an attempt to curtail self-doubt, I fill all the paperwork out quickly—and honestly. (I am thankfully not a chronic overthinker.) At this point, I'm already picturing myself going through the docuseries' official matchmaking process. This could be my chance at finding love. A buoy in the rough waters of dating. A lifeboat.

I tell myself not to get my hopes up.

The next day, the call goes smoothly. It's casual and laid-back. Relieved, I move on with my workday. Early the next week, I receive another email. There was a glitch in the previous call and audio wasn't recorded. But they enjoyed the conversation with me. Would I mind doing it again? I agree. Of course I do. Being single is like being stranded. I don't want to be stranded.

Another call is set up with a second member of the casting team. After that one also goes smoothly, she reaches out to schedule a third call—this time with my sister, my mother, and me. It feels . . . fast. I hadn't expected fast. It's only been two weeks since I first sent the email expressing interest in the Facebook post. Gosh, I'd been in L.A. when I did that! Feeling defeated.

But fast is good, I tell myself. *Fast is what I need.*

After the interview with my family, I'm asked if my mother will do a solo interview on Skype. She agrees, a time is set—but then the casting team writes to reschedule the interview due to an emergency. After that, they fall silent. No communication. No response. I feel deflated. It looks like the boat won't stop for me, after all. Like Jack in *Titanic*, I am slowly sinking into the sea. At least Jack had Rose.

I give up on the show, assuming they've moved on. My friends ask me about it every now and then, and I shrug noncommittally. *I didn't make the cut*, I tell them. To myself I add: *The lifeboat didn't have room for me.*

With the holidays fast approaching, I hit the dating scene through apps with new fervor. On the other side of Christmas is my January birthday. In my world, being thirty-four and single would verge on spinsterhood. I have two months to find someone.

I commit to checking each dating app at least twice a day. I figure out a new, more efficient strategy heading into the new year. I'll schedule a date at 6:30 PM at a wine bar that closes at 8:00 PM, and then a second date at 8:00 PM down the street, where I'll sign off by 10:00 PM, citing work early the next morning. Dates will be only two days a week, Monday to Wednesday, to ensure that no one can insist I stay longer on a Thursday by exclaiming, *But tomorrow is Friday. Let's have another drink.*

And it works. In an "A-for-effort" sort of way.

Think about it: even if I line up four dates, I still have five nights of the week for friends, family, long workouts, or just sitting on the couch and lounging. It's a new-and-improved way to tackle the task of dating. (And yes, that's how I see dating at this age—as a task. That's how any South Asian woman sees it when she's fast approaching her thirty-fourth birthday.) An efficient approach is a smart approach. I've always been good at planning, at meeting my goals. Finding love is my goal.

One time, I almost get caught. A 6:30 PM'er announces he's going to meet his friends after our date. He is texting as we grab the check—I do the fake reach and he waves my hand aside—and casually notes that they are headed to the same bar as my 8:00 PM'er. I jump in with an anecdote about how parking is a nightmare. And did he know that the bar's drinks are always overly sweet? (Mind you, this bar is famously known for its craft cocktails.) One of my rambling distastes for the bar must have resonated, because he shoots off a group text with a new location. *Thanks for looking out for me,* he says. I smile sweetly and hurry along to date number two. Crisis averted.

Look, I never said my approach was perfect. I still stand by it, though. Efficiency is key. Even if it comes with its hiccups and white lies.

Two months later, in December 2018, I receive a casting email. More important, they're "still very much interested" and are "working to get everything in order for the network pitch." We set up a call.

Hope bubbles in my chest. Could there be a spot for me on the lifeboat after all? Am I no longer destined to drown in the sea of dating in Houston?

On the phone, a team member assures me they are moving forward with the show. Am I still interested in going through the vetting process?

For me, this is a chance. A chance to follow a proper process, to bring some clarity to the elusive question of why I haven't met my life partner yet. Maybe, just maybe, the Universe needs to make my own meet-cute from my beloved romantic comedies a camera-worthy moment. Maybe I've always been destined to find love in such a unique way. Every other way has failed me so far.

I say yes. Of course I say yes.

I wait patiently. OK, that's a lie. But I do *wait*. What choice do I have?

Two months later, I hear back.

It's a yes. Sort of.

I'll be on the show, they tell me, but only *if* I pass the background check and the psychological evaluation.

My heart does a celebratory somersault. I'm not worried; I don't have a criminal record. And I appreciate that they're asking cast members to undergo a psychological evaluation. It lends the process an air of credibility. I eagerly send in my background forms, including my address for the last five years, a copy of my Texas driver's license, and, of course, a copy of my US naturalization certificate.

The lifeboat has never felt so close.

In March 2019, six months after my first contact, I shut my office door to log into Skype. I have a meeting with a psychologist. Clear, insightful, and direct in his speech, the doctor shares that life will be different after the show launches. People will think they know me. People will come up to me in stores and restaurants, on airplanes and in restrooms even, to tell me their opinion on my choices of men on the show. I can't help but laugh. This isn't *The Bachelor*, I remind him. He quickly agrees that this is not in his traditional wheelhouse of more risqué dating shows.

I still remember the day I am told I am officially on the show: March 12, 2019. I am no longer referred to as an applicant but rather as part of the show in an email with a real-life producer. I'm thrilled! Gone are the *if* clauses, the sentences in the conditional tense. I'm in. Present tense. And as I converse with these producers, it dawns on me: I've made it. The screening process is behind me.

In that moment, I envision myself boarding the lifeboat, clutching on to the raft's rubbery sides, steadying myself on its wobbly floors. In the distance I can spot my destination: a matchmaker who will find the most perfect partner *for me*. My heart soars. For the first time in a long time, my romantic future looks promising.

At this point, you're probably wondering, *What's with the lifeboat metaphor?*

Well, here's the thing: it's not a metaphor. Or it is, but it's also more than that. In my thirty-six years on this Earth, lifeboats—both literal and figurative—have shaped the woman I am and, consequently, the way I live.

You see, *Indian Matchmaking* wasn't my first time on a lifeboat. That happened fifteen years earlier.

My first boat was actually a ship—one that I lived on for one hundred days in my junior year of college. That ship represented many things. A home. The thing on which I pinned my independence. An outlet for my wanderlust, for my lifelong love of travel. Most of all, it rescued me from predictability, from a mundane routine and a lifetime without finding my only true love to date: travel.

So this ship, too, was a lifeboat. A lifeboat that I had to fight to get on.

The program is called Semester at Sea. The elevator pitch for Semester at Sea promised *a study abroad program that acted as a floating university for students to circumnavigate the globe, visiting ten countries in one hundred days.* In other words, college on a boat. What's not to love about that?

I'd first been exposed to the college-on-a-boat concept when I watched *Road Rules*, a popular '90s MTV show that followed six college students exploring the world through its various ports. I was never one of those kids who had to be bribed or coaxed out of watching TV. Books have always been my passion. But every Tuesday afternoon, I'd prop myself on my living room's carpeted floor, cross my legs, and widen my eyes. I spent the next thirty minutes mesmerized by the ecstatic, adventurous teens on screen. I decided that would be me someday.

A goal without a plan is a wish. And I am—and have always been—a planner.

Five years later, in my sophomore year of college, I visited my university's study abroad office. I scanned the rows of colorful brochures against the wall—Italy, Samoa, Ghana. Pictures of rocky, seaside cliffs and magenta sunsets. No ship option. No Semester at Sea.

I approached the frumpy woman with glasses perched on her nose. Where could I learn about the Semester at Sea program?

"No, dear," she said, her face furrowing like an amused chipmunk. "We don't support that program at this university."

It was my turn to furrow my brow—*un*amused. "Could you look into it for me?"

Sadly, she could not. "If you want to go, you'll have to take a leave of absence," she explained. In a fatalistic tone, she added, "Your scholarships and grants won't transfer, and you won't get any credit."

Perhaps sensing my deflated expression, she added, "May I suggest a semester in London?"

Her advice felt like an insult. *London*? Here I was asking about a program that would take me to *ten countries*, and this woman thought that I'd be satisfied with a trip to my birth city? (Yes, I'm aware she didn't know I was born in London—no one ever assumes that looking at me, but I was still peeved.) I didn't want a sedentary semester in *one* country. I wanted ten countries. Ten!

I asked to speak to the dean of the study abroad program.

Chipmunk told me it was pointless. The dean's answer would be the same as hers. She was done giving me unsolicited advice at this point. She no longer seemed amused, just annoyed.

I shared her annoyance. But I wasn't about to give up. When I was younger, my grandmother—my Nani—taught me that a *no* is just the starting point in a negotiation.

And negotiate I did.

I made phone calls. I wrote emails. Formal letters. I appealed the school's decision to not accept the program because it didn't create enough "immersion into one specific culture." (Was *the world* not cultural enough for them?) I got approval from the financial aid office to transfer my scholarships. I allowed the school to select my classes onboard the ship. I jumped through every hoop they threw my way.

Hoping to gain an advocate for my cause, I spoke to a Rice University professor who had taught on the ship eight years prior. He was a chatty sort, full of run-on anecdotes and vague stories about his faculty days on Semester at Sea. He spoke of the *five lost in India to the accident en route to the Taj Mahal* and how difficult it was to sail away from that port without them. It took another thirty minutes for him to reveal that *lost* was a euphemism for *dead*. Five students had tragically passed away in an accident when a tour driver attempted to dodge a bad pothole on the highway. I'll admit, in that moment, a spike of fear shot up my spine. Once again, I thought of Nani. She never let fear stop her. I wasn't about to, either. I remained steadfast in my ambition. That wouldn't happen to me. That was an accident. Accidents could even happen in London, I rationalized.

And it paid off—weeks after my first conversation with Chipmunk, I'd convinced the university. Semester at Sea was a go.

I didn't know it then, but I was about to embark on a transformative experience. Or maybe I did know it. Maybe that's why I fought so hard to get on that boat. Because who remains unchanged after seeing the world?

Picture a twenty-year-old Aparna facing the ship. It was a hot day in August 2005. I was at a port in Nassau, wearing a sheer brown knit tank with a short, faded red chambray skirt, which, to my mind at the time, represented the height of "ship chic." In reality, it was woefully inappropriate—the winds on the upper decks blew strongly. Eight hundred other kids from American universities— and me!—trickled aboard the relatively tiny seven-story ship. I couldn't stop craning my neck, taking it all in. My skin tingled with excitement and anticipation. I'd never been on a cruise before, and this was rumored to be the fastest passenger ship in the world. It had been bought from a bankrupt Greek cruise company and had antiquated quotes from Greek philosophers randomly splattered on the walls. The old bar had been turned into a library. Conference rooms became classrooms. And we were expected to share our miniscule cabins with a random stranger.

It was college on a boat. It was an adventure—the adventure I'd longed for since I was fifteen years old.

Mara, my roommate, was a beautiful, tan, large-eyed girl from Maryland who became my safe haven. She was full of life advice. I had to wear eyeliner, she explained. And would I like to join her in lifting free weights four times a week to stay toned? Together, we danced around the room listening to the local music of countries we'd visit. We traded life stories, whispered confessions in the dark. Mara was fun. In fact, fun was her specialty. Naturally, I was grateful. A fun roommate goes hand in hand with college on a boat.

But I was also desperately homesick—both for my family and for the life I'd left behind.

I'd spent so much time planning my semester abroad that I'd never given any thought to the semester I'd be missing out on. The one on land, back in Texas. Back in my real life. But now it sunk in: my Rice friends were living their lives, following the comforting routines we had built together—from 8:00 AM golf classes with Starbucks on the way to the driving range, to planning our costumes for the weekly theme parties on campus, to giggling over which guy made a fool of himself on Thursday night at the campus pub. Except now, they were doing it all *without me*.

And it's not that the ship wasn't great. It was.

Day after day, I had the ocean as my backyard. At night, I had hypnotizing starry skies. I had a community to explore: at any moment, I could strike up a conversation with a stranger and make friends with a fellow globally minded student.

But I also had FOMO. And motion sickness. Believe me when I say this is *not* a good combination—there's something about constantly throwing up that makes you miss home even more. We were all on malaria drugs too. In hindsight, I wonder if the drugs didn't wreak havoc in our emotions. Side effects stated on the medication bottles and pamphlets included "suicidal thoughts and hallucinations." At the time, I didn't factor that into the equation. All I knew is that I had a case of the blues. It didn't help that internet costs were prohibitive and cell phone service (if you could afford it) was erratic. Back then, in 2005, cell phones did not work worldwide—and certainly not in the middle of an ocean.

I wanted an adventure. But the truth is that I hadn't given any real thought to the cost of that adventure. At least not beyond the dollar amount.

Still, the ship went on. It didn't care that my heart was homesick, and for that I was grateful. I was there to keep on moving. To explore.

Our first stop was Venezuela. We landed in La Guaira only four days after leaving Nassau. I was eager to spend time off the ship, to buy a newspaper and find out what had happened while I was at sea. But before we disembarked, a few names were called out over the speaker—six, maybe seven names in total. Ripples of questions erupted between us. Why were these students being summoned? They weren't related to each other, so it couldn't have been a family emergency. I remember Mara asking me if I had any idea what was going on. I didn't. None of us did. Speculation buzzed among us, that low-level excitement that comes with the unknown.

Except, as we would soon learn, there was nothing to be excited about. Just the opposite, in fact.

Tragedy had struck.

A hurricane called Katrina had broken the New Orleans levies and totaled towns on the southeastern Gulf coastline. The names we heard over the intercom belonged to students whose homes had been destroyed. They were to fly home. And the misfortune didn't stop there. Another student, James, was called over the intercom as well. James had no connections to New Orleans. Instead, he was summoned because his father had passed away. He flew out that evening with the Katrina group. Collective grief spread among us like spilled oil.

This wasn't how any of us had envisioned our adventure. I personally hadn't realized the heaviness of leaving behind life at home—and the cost of being physically and technologically removed from information. I felt shocked. While we had been cementing new friendships over personal pan pizzas on Deck Seven, a hurricane had been flattening towns in the southern United States, flooding New Orleans. And then there was the fresh notion that someone's parent could suddenly pass away with no warning, no foresight. Would James come back? Would he give up this semester to stay close to his remaining family? What would I do if I were in his shoes? Would I give this all up?

And yet, with the world still turning, Venezuela was waiting for us. Mara and I parted ways, and I—along with thirty other students—traveled to a magical mountain town called Mérida. Our pit stop along the way was at the Maria Lionza cult center on Sorte Mountain. This cult was a mix of Indigenous, African, and Catholic beliefs. We arrived at dusk to the sound of beating drums that reverberated through my pounding heart. We smoked cigars with local gatherers amused by visitors to this remote spot. Army guards traveling with us to our final destination accompanied us through the throngs of people. They led us up the mountain, stopping at each shrine created by families, witnessing what appeared to be sacrificial goats and young girls dressed in white, as well as hearty celebrations of unions resembling weddings.

In total, we spent four days in Venezuela. Four days where I journeyed through the Andes Mountains, rappelled down rocky, cliffside waterfalls, and slept uncomfortably on overnight buses to get to our next location. I paid twenty dollars to paraglide through the valleys at sunset—the sky turning pink, then purple, then dark blue as I floated through the horizon. I remember it was a Tuesday, the day I saw the world from a dusk-colored rainbow sky. A Tuesday where I would have otherwise been eating a cold dinner in the cafeteria at school. Instead I was flying over the Venezuelan foothills.

It was an incredible experience. And yet, in the back of my mind, I couldn't stop thinking of my classmates who had flown back home.

What does it mean that every single one of those students came back before we left the La Guaira port? I like to think that it means the ocean had bonded us. That we weren't about to let anything—not a destructive hurricane, not a terrible death—keep us from forging ahead, from living our adventure. We were wanderers. And we were in it together.

I had found my people.

We forged onward. Brazil came next—the split city of Salvador, Bahia. I remember being on the ship's deck with James, overlooking Bay of All Saints with its coral reefs and tropical vegetation. We'd struck up a conversation hours before our arrival and, in that moment, as we took in the blue-green water, he told me something I'll never forget.

"My dad would've loved this place," he said, his voice almost a whisper.

There was a long pause. "I'm sorry for your loss," I said, finally. Words seemed insufficient.

He gave me a sad smile. "He would've wanted me to be here." His tone was filled with conviction. He went on to explain that his father had been excited for his son's semester at sea. How many people got to attend university aboard a ship? How many people got to travel for one hundred days? I could relate, at least in part. My mom had been excited for me too. Though I couldn't begin to imagine the pain I'd feel if I lost her. That's when it dawned on me: *This is truly a once-in-a-lifetime opportunity. Not just for me. Not just for James. But for all of us.*

I couldn't succumb to homesickness or seasickness. I had to make it count.

And make it count I did—in Salvador, Bahia. I learned about the city, about its oldest public transportation: an elevator that took locals from the Lower City to the Upper City. About the numerous churches: one for every day of the year with a few more to spare. Conga lines and percussionists ruled the nights fueled by caipirinhas and mojitos. This country brought me into first contact with the group of fellow students from the ship I would later call my best friends. Separated from Mara for most of the day due to class schedules and different mealtimes, I had expanded my social circle and was slowly finding people I bonded with and related to quickly and intimately.

I didn't know it then, but I wasn't just exploring the world. Slowly but surely, I was making my own family. The people who would, years later, invite me to officiate their weddings. The people I'd count on when I went through heartbreak and sorrow. The people whose babies I'd hold and love in our thirties.

As I stood on a colorful cobblestone street in Salvador, it struck me that *this* was the way I wanted to see the world. This was my way out of the small pond I lived in at Rice University—one that was ruled by how many boys I kissed or what I wore to the last costume party or whether I would win an election to be president of a club. There, I was drowning in pleasing people.

Here, I was seeing a world bigger than anything I had imagined existed.

In that moment, I felt deep gratitude toward the ship, the vessel that would take me around the world to show me how big this globe is but also how interconnected we all are as people.

Was I cured of homesickness? No, of course not. I thought about my friends back home all the time, often while a sadness swelled inside my heart. But my homesickness was no longer in control. It was a constant, a passenger in the lifeboat with me. But I was at the front of the boat. I was rowing the oars. I was propelling the boat forward.

Life was just beginning for me. And it was all because of this ship.

The ship sailed on to South Africa. This stretch in the journey was rough: the waves were high and oh-so constant, leaving me temporarily regretting the decision to ever put myself through this physical discomfort. Never-ending stomach turns and wretches over a sink became a way of life. There were moments when I'd pray for sleep to stop the constant rocking motion—a futile hope, because the motion continued even in sleep. This was especially challenging because I wasn't on vacation, I was a full-time student. Learning on the boat felt impossible with these physical limitations, but it had to be done. The program was composed of a strict fifty-day period of classes onboard the ship and another fifty days in countries, for one hundred days total. Slacking was not tolerated.

Here's what made it better: Desmond Tutu and his wife were with us for the nine days that we journeyed across the Atlantic Ocean. Yes, Desmond Tutu.

Global studies was a mandatory class, but with Desmond Tutu on board it felt like a privilege. We all trickled in to listen to his stories of apartheid and his role in the Truth and Reconciliation Commission of South Africa. I had breakfast one morning with him and his wife along with four other students. Over lumpy scrambled eggs and orange juice, we discussed the Partition of India. He patiently listened as I recounted how my family members suffered one of two fates: we either managed to leave with very little in the middle of the night or had been killed trying to flee what is now modern-day Pakistan. He was a worldly, cultured man, but he was also hopeful and optimistic. He saw humanity's capacity to grieve and forgive as limitless. It was beautiful.

After visiting the township of Khayelitsha, Robben Island, and the famed District Six Museum, I was heartened to see the strength of the South African people in uniting in the face of what many would call insurmountable collective pain. This trip was healing wounds I didn't know I had. It was giving me faith—faith in humanity and in the ability of recognizing each other without the definition of skin color. I remember thinking that Desmond Tutu's optimism was rubbing off on me.

And then, on my last night there, my roommate and I joined a group of girls to check out the nightlife in Cape Town. We stood in line at a club called Maverick, waiting impatiently for the bouncer to acknowledge us. While crowds of people got in, he left us standing to the side without a glance our way. Mara, arguably the beauty of our group, finally approached him. If I close my eyes, I can picture her standing across from him.

"Excuse me?" Mara asked, politely. "We've been waiting here for fifteen minutes. We are Americans visiting Cape Town and would love to come in for a few drinks."

He surveyed us, visibly unimpressed. "*They* can come in." He pointed to two of our friends—Julia and Gwen.

"Well, we are all together," Mara replied, confusion evident in her tone.

"There are four of us," Julia said. Then, in a hopeful tone, she added. "No men in our group."

That would have worked stateside. Here, he was nonplussed.

"OK. But you two have to pay." He paused and looked at Julia and Gwen again, "They can come in."

We all stood back, confused. I could tell his words made no sense to any of us. Why would Gwen and Julia be allowed in but not Mara and me?

And then the obvious hit me.

Julia and Gwen were both blondes with blue eyes.

My gorgeous roommate had legs for days and the brightest smile in the room. But she also had chocolate brown eyes and dark brown hair. And me? Well, I wasn't just a Caucasian brunette with olive skin—I was South Asian. My instincts told me that, to this man, my worth was even less.

Indignation rose in my throat. I took another step back.

Mara and I exchanged a glance. At age twenty, in a foreign country, we weren't in the mood for a fight. We didn't want to make a scene. Besides, our two other friends had already sashayed inside. Wordlessly, we agreed to let it go.

Mara paid ten rand to the bouncer.

I had to pay thirty. (My instincts were right.)

I walked in last, dazed and unsure of what I'd find at this club. The bouncer's friend loitering inside spit on the ground next to me. I looked up with a start.

He curled his lip and snarled, "Why don't you go back to the township you've come from?" He seemed disgusted by my presence at the club. Repulsed.

Looking back, I wasn't just startled. I was scared too. So scared I didn't respond.

I hurried inside to catch up with my friends. I didn't mention this to any of them. Not even Mara.

This wasn't the first time I'd come face-to-face with South African racism. There had been uncomfortable moments in the Stellenbosch wine region a few days prior when I visited

with Katelin, my best friend from Rice who was coinciden-
tally studying in Cape Town, but we chalked it up to it being
a more rural Afrikaans community. Sure, they expressed displeasure at Katelin with her strawberry blond hair and green
eyes walking in with me to their tastings. Sure, they followed
me carefully—vigilantly—through the cellars. Sure, they seated
us in the back corners of their main tasting rooms. And it
didn't feel good. Of course it didn't. But I had already decided
to ignore those microaggressions. There was so much to love
about this gorgeous country—wine lands, penguins on beaches,
and terrain that inspired explorers in generations past. Plus, I
was still imbued by the faith Desmond Tutu had instilled in
me aboard the ship.

But this at the club—this was too much.

I now understood that South Africa, for all its natural beauty,
was not a country that welcomed me. I was left with a bad taste
in my mouth. More than that, I was left heartbroken.

I missed home. Heartbreak makes us crave the familiar. In
that moment, my homesickness took the oars from my hands as I
shrunk back, wounded. I didn't have it in me to steer the lifeboat.

Later, I learned to talk about my experiences with racism in
South Africa. I would even tell Shekar about this on our first
date on *Indian Matchmaking* when he voiced his desire to visit.
I always caution South Asians who travel there. I share my 2005
experiences, reveal the racist undertones constantly directed at me
throughout my visit, and advise them to consider this potential
treatment if and when they ever visit.

Personally, I choose to take my tourism dollars to communities
that are welcoming to visitors. The world is too big, and I am
too practical, to subject myself to that kind of behavior, especially when on holiday. South Africa taught me that travel isn't
always emotionally comfortable and that sometimes your own

experience will color how you view a country. It's personal. And I was truly saddened to leave such a natural paradise without saying, "I'll be back soon." Countries are like people—they can break your heart.

But then some countries surprise you.

Our next collective surprise was waiting for us when we returned to the ship after seven days in Cape Town. Semester at Sea has a very strict policy for departures. If you aren't on board by the indicated time, you are left on the dock and can either go home or fly to the next port and meet the ship there. I barely made this port call, and when I did, I received the news that we would not be headed to Kenya next as planned. The program's risk assessment team had been warned that if we attempted to dock in Mombasa, a terrorist group would bomb our ship.

As I heard those words—*terrorist group* and *bomb our ship*—I felt my stomach sink in fear. Still, I tried to keep it together. It was an adventure I wanted. Adventures included risks. Risks included bomb threats, or so I told myself. Although, in the hum of the voices around me as we gathered in the main square on the ship, I wondered what would have happened if no "tip" had been given to our risk assessment team. What would have happened to these people milling around? To me? Would we be the next formidable tale at any university when a student requested to go on Semester at Sea? Quickly I realized if any such thing happened, there would never again be a Semester at Sea.

In an attempt to stay calm, I inquired as to what our Plan B might be. Surely, I'd feel better once I knew where we were headed. Somewhere beautiful and exotic and terrorist-free.

Except, as it turned out, there was no Plan B. We were stuck with nowhere to go.

Calls were made to different countries with frantic negotiations. As it turned out, not every port city is eager to accept eight hundred Americans (and a few world citizens like myself—I had an Indian passport at the time) with no visas. It took almost eighteen hours for us to find a new temporary home.

We were to head to the island country of Mauritius.

If you have to pause to look up Mauritius on your phone, go ahead. You'll hear no judgment from me—95 percent of the ship's population had never heard of Mauritius, which, quite frankly, is a shame. More people should know about it. I had family friends from Mauritius who had left many years prior and moved to London. I had long heard stories of this paradise.

Mauritius welcomed us with open arms—and, more important, no restrictions.

Just like that, we all experienced a slice of heaven on earth for the next four days. I watched Hindu pilgrims walk the length of the island for a religious holiday, zip-lined through sugarcane plantations, hiked rough trails for the reward of a nature's bath in a waterfall, and had blissfully bouncer-free nightlife adventures with friends until the wee hours of the morning. There is a certain beauty to traveling at age twenty—your energy is limitless. You can wake up at 6:00 AM for tours and adventures and stay out drinking fruity cocktails until 4:00 AM. And then do it again. And again. For a week at a time!

Every port was spring break with a heavy dose of cultural activities. Every day on the ship became a recovery that consisted of sleep, curing whatever common ailment you picked up—which typically ranged from a cough to a sprained ankle—and trying to make it through your classes and assignments. Yes, we had homework. We had midterms and finals. We had mandatory field trips—except these weren't like any others. They were to water-falls in Brazil, townships in South Africa, memorial museums in Hiroshima, and monasteries in Myanmar.

Mauritius was our pause, our break. Our very own literal and figurative surprise. I never thought I'd see a silver lining in a terrorist threat, but I did. In a manner of speaking.

Onward to India! Our fifth of ten countries and a halfway point where we reached Asia.

I had my friend group solidified and was excited about showing off my favorite destination. I planned two days with my family, who invited my friends and me to stay as guests, and three days in a rural village in South India. I made the choice early on to pick excursions and trips I knew I wouldn't have access to in the one-day far-off future, like in my thirties.

The village stay consisted of an overnight train in first class with plastic beds covered in stiffly pressed, stained sheets. When the lights were turned off and we were timidly settled into our bunks, I heard the squeaking of rodents inches from my face scurrying along the train floor. I screamed. My fellow bottom bunk roommate screamed. Within minutes, we were huddled on the top bunks for the rest of the night with two other classmates. First class, indeed!

Exhausted, we reached our home for the next two days. Lunch was served off banana leaves on the floor. The food was delicious and authentic. As I nibbled on dosas and figured out how to dive into the sambar without a spoon (you sip from the bowl, I learned), I thought to myself, *I can do this*. I was excited for my stay. The day was spent visiting coconut farms where we witnessed the picking of the fruit and then its husking. We went on to visit a special education school and then a local watering hole.

I felt a surge of pride: I was living my own life. I was not in a cushy hotel. I was not with family—I was battling down trains with vermin and taking on rural India by myself. Or so I told myself until I went to the restroom in the middle of the night, pulling myself off my mattress on the floor lined up with twelve others in the room and turning on the lights to see hundreds of the mightiest black ants crawling all over the commode. Stifling a scream so as to not wake everyone, I waited until the light dissipated them into the corners and drains and hovered as best as I could. There was no toilet paper—only a water jug. I had, after all, asked for the "authentic experience," so pink plastic wash jug it was.

To this day, my family still laughs at me for what they call my *harebrained travel notions.* I understand their amusement, but the truth is that I'd do it all over again if I could. I'd never take back those experiences. Since then, I've stayed in five-star hotels in India many times, and none have had quite the same charm. They weren't adventures. They weren't unexpected. And the only new thing I learned in those luxury stays was which international food station I preferred in the never-ending breakfast buffets.

Leaving India, we sped onward to Myanmar in an effort to ward off the pirates who loiter in the Indian Ocean. At the ship's highest knots and within twenty-four hours, we were in the untouched land of child monks, an ever-watchful government, and the most serene countryside I've ever seen. In a place where it appeared that pagodas outnumbered people, we discovered beauty that had not been touched by tourism. I fell in love with seeing something so new. I hadn't read about it much—it wasn't in my history books and it sure wasn't covered as a travel destination in glossy magazines. I wanted more of this, of that I was certain.

Before Myanmar, I would stand on the edge of the fifth-level deck of the ship every night after my workout and stretch my arm out over the railing. In those moments, I comforted myself knowing I was the closest person to home. I was so grounded in my identity at home that I felt like I was floating with no control over my direction without it. By the time we entered the Arabian Sea, standing on the back of the ship only made me the farthest from home. A quick flip—both in logistical geography and in my mind.

In Vietnam, I found unbridled joy. In hindsight, it was likely because I learned for the first time to appreciate what was right in front of me instead of what was back home. Until then, whenever my ribs constricted in longing—for my family, for my friends—I reminded myself of what I'd be missing out on if I weren't here, in this journey around the world. That was my strategy: using FOMO to combat homesickness, fear to fight longing.

All that changed in Vietnam.

I can replay the scene in my mind with perfect clarity. There I was, in Ho Chi Minh, perched atop a stool in a tiny internet café blaring '90s pop music. Facebook had launched its photograph section the day before—this was November 2005. As the desktop computer's screen flooded with my friends' pictures from the latest costume party, I felt my heart sink. My friends looked perfect. Perfect smiles. Glamorous outfits. Chic poses. They looked like what they were: young college students having the time of their lives. In contrast, I was literally covered in grime from the city's dirt and pollution. My hair was pulled back in a messy ponytail, and I was wearing a two-dollar T-shirt I'd bought on a whim at a Burmese market the week prior. The dingy café had a rusty mirror, which meant that I could see myself for what I was: *un*glamorous and *un*chic. Nothing like my friends. Nothing like the woman I used to be.

And that's when it hit me. I was nothing like the woman I used to be. I'd changed.

The realization felt like lightning, instant and sharp.

I had a choice to make.

I could wallow and throw myself a pity party because my tiny world back home was spinning just fine without me. Or I could shift my perspective and realize that this was my chance to live life on my own lifeboat. It was my very opportunity to exist—*successfully* exist—away from the people I loved.

I chose the latter.

I shut off the computer, paid my Vietnamese dong fees at the checkout counter, and waited outside as my friends finished sending emails home. I stood on the street corner of a new, unfamiliar city, watching hundreds of people pass me by on motorbikes, foot, rickshaws, and bicycles. The city was alive, thrumming. A living thing imbued by the elixir of constant motion. Everyone here was moving—always moving.

I vowed to do the same.

That day, homesickness left the lifeboat altogether. It never came back.

Vietnam was breathtaking. Perhaps any place that grants you personal freedom will be your favorite. For me, it was a country where I walked misty rice paddy fields, slept in a long house in a rural village full of silk artisans, and drank cold beers on the edge of "town," eight hours north of Hanoi. In Ho Chi Minh, I ran the infamous Cu Chi tunnels—breathing hard as I sprinted through the remnants of guerilla warfare bunkers underground, seeing the shells of operating rooms and weapons caches, imagining the world that lived down there during the Vietnam War (fittingly called the American War by the Vietnamese). I was so free in those days: laughing loudly on the back of motorbikes, buying Tiger Beer T-shirts en masse, and solidifying lifelong friendships.

Looking back, Vietnam was the beginning of my independence from worrying about what others were saying or doing in the world. If my world was good, if the waters around me were to my liking—whether excitingly choppy or gloriously still—then I was where I had to be.

I was at peace. I was unstoppable.

The Asian destinations sped by too quickly.

China. I traveled to the "Gumdrop hills" of Guilin, a poetic place where fog clings to the oddly beautiful hills, mystical and otherworldly.

Hong Kong. In 2005, the British exit of 1997 was still felt in the daily melting pot of urban living there—my cosmopolitan food stops consisting of not only Marks & Spencer but also dim sum and California Pizza Kitchen. America does have a special way of inviting itself into a country's casual cuisine.

Japan. Our last stop—and one of revelry. The carefree, youthful decision of getting matching tattoos with my friends topped the list of "flying high." Not realizing the Japanese stigma against tattoos due to their historical ties to gang-related activities, we searched the streets asking everyone for a tattoo parlor. We also clutched napkins asking strangers to write down the characters for "the world," so we could compare them before the inking started. We were met with rush-hour commuters who were too polite to say no but were still perfectly capable of conveying their distaste for our American ways. (Nowadays, this would've been so much easier with GPS!)

Finally, we found a shop selling marijuana-illustrated bumper stickers. The people there knew one tattoo parlor and drew us a simple map of the Kobe neighborhood. Two rights and one left later, we were standing in front of an alleyway where a neon light lit up the name of the parlor: THANK YOU VERY DADDY. Napkins in hand, we went one by one—everyone else got their tattoo on their foot, so it would be visible in flip-flops and in heels. I was a little more reticent and got mine on "my heart." Years later, I would forget about my "tit-oo" until I caught glimpse of it in the shower. Always a smile for this tiny, two-centimeter impression of "the world."

The voyage ended after a one-day pit stop in Hawaii on the way back to the States. We said our tearful goodbyes and promised to be friends forever.

I am proud to report that, as promised, we are just that.

But why am I telling you all this?

Surely, you picked up this book because you "met" me on *Indian Matchmaking*. You wanted to know what made me go on a reality show. What I've been doing since. How my life has changed since I was cast on a show as a difficult woman. An unlikeable villain. A shrew (such a dumb word).

Well, the answer to that has to do with that trip, with that journey around the world.

Over the course of those one hundred days on the ship, where I slowly and surely gained my sea legs (albeit with heavy doses of motion sickness), I also gained an important life lesson: I could do it.

I, Aparna Shewakramani, could do it.

Whatever *it* the future held in store for me, I could find my own way through it. Just as I'd pulled myself out of desperate homesickness. Just as I'd overcome blatant racism in a country where I'd hoped to heal. Whatever the obstacle, the change, the challenge.

I. Could. Do. It.

Seeing ten countries with ten cultures and infinite subcultures in a short span of time showed me that the world was smaller than I had ever imagined. We were all connected. And the best part was this: I still had a lot more to see.

And after my adventure, I knew that I wouldn't be seeing it from a beach cabana or an all-inclusive resort. I would be seeing it like this—with adventure, spirit, and eyes wide open.

I'd face it all. Because I was stronger than it all.

Little did I know that my strength would be put to the test in the summer of 2017, when I got on yet another lifeboat. This time, literally.

The call arrived on Sunday, August 27, 2017.

I answered the phone groggy and irritable—it wasn't even 7:00 AM yet. My uncle was on the other end of the line, frantic. Hurricane Harvey was coming our way. I assured him we were fine. I hung up, still annoyed. Looking back, my naïveté frightens me; I didn't think we were in danger.

I was wrong.

As soon as I looked out the window, I saw it: the water level rising over the cars' tires in the driveway. I still didn't believe it would enter the house, but I sprang into action. Better safe than sorry. The real challenge was that my mom had limited mobility— she'd had her hip replaced two weeks prior and was using a walker to get around. This meant we couldn't simply walk (or swim) away.

I moved pictures from the bottom shelves. I threw everything from the floor level onto beds and shelves. My mother packed a duffel bag of important documents, dog food, and medicines. I rushed throughout the house trying to rescue what was below the four-foot mark—if the water rose higher than that, what was the use of trying to save anything?

The dogs were frantic. Unable to go outside, they were barking to use the bathroom. I tried to get them to relieve themselves inside, but they refused. They were livid, mostly at me, as if I were causing the flood. And then, it happened. The water seeped in from under the doors. I hurried to get duct tape. In hindsight, that's laughable. Tape was not going to save us. Nor were the towels I threw on the floor, emptying the linen closet to cover the front and back doors. Soon the water was rising to cover the entire house and the rain outside was pelting down with no respite.

Nervously, I looked at my mother and her huge wound. I assessed the water outside to be about three or four feet high, with the current pushing debris and piles of ants clinging to each other for survival past the window.

The water was toxic—class 4. We knew that much.

We had to get out of the house. We knew that too.

Swimming wasn't an option. We had the dogs, and my mom had a fresh wound. Frantic WhatsApp messages were sent out to my friend groups. A Facebook post was shared around town asking for independent rescues. My boss tweeted to FEMA, requesting a medical necessity rescue for my mother.

No one came.

The water continued to rise: inches at first, and then a full foot.

Images of CNN's coverage of Hurricane Katrina crept into my head, striking panic about the rising waters inside the house. People standing on roofs, helicopters saving the lucky ones. I remembered the stories of folks going into their attics and drowning once the waters rose to the roof. Even an ax can't ensure your way out if you're in the attic. The television ran in the background echoing warnings even as we debated when we had to turn it off to avoid a house fire. All I could think of was *I have to get my mom and the dogs out of here.*

I called the Houston Police Department. After hours on hold, they told me they couldn't help me because, technically, I didn't live in Houston (I lived in a small city *within* Houston—Bellaire). Their advice was to climb to my roof, but again from the outside.

Now I could barely breathe. I called the City of Bellaire—it was past 2:00 PM.

"Why didn't you call sooner?" they asked. "We will not be able to get to you today. We are backed up, so you need to find an alternative."

They suggested hanging out the window and asking for help. They also suggested making a sign for the window to signal that we had been rescued—to leave there once we got out.

Were we going to get out? I had to believe we were.

We made a sign by scribbling with a Sharpie on the back of an old poster board.

I opened the window and saw an empty street with a fast current moving east. The sun was out, and I knew this was our short respite before the torrential rains resumed. A woman waded by on the far side of the street. She looked to be about my age, carrying a dog on her shoulders, fighting the current as it hit her mid-hip. I called out to her to ask if she had seen boats. She hadn't but hollered that the neighbors from our street were at the high school. It was only half a block away. I explained why we couldn't swim there because of my mom and asked if she could keep an eye out for rescue crews. She wished us luck and waded on. It was another twenty minutes before an older woman on a red, one-person kayak moved quickly past us, a young Black man perched on the nose as she moved him to safety. She didn't hear me call out to her. She was too focused on getting the balancing man to higher ground.

No one else came. It was almost 4:00 PM, and the sky was darkening with heavy clouds again. The woman in her kayak returned from the direction in which she had been going. I called out to her again, desperation in my voice. She was our only hope. I explained the situation and swam out there myself, in a peach dress and rain boots. Snakes splashed next to me, and I stifled the urge to scream as my dress floated around me. Pants. Why hadn't I worn pants?

We introduced each other. Her name was Barb. Barb escaped her home by the bayou two miles away to come shelter in place with her friend. And then her friend's house flooded. She was currently on her way back to her home (she'd forgotten her documents), and then she was headed to a shelter. I looked up again at the clouds—how could I ask her to help us when she had her own race against Mother Nature? But I had to.

And Barb agreed—quickly, unthinkingly.

Her first instinct was to say yes to my plea. To help me.

We paddled toward my house. Barb instructed me to push the front door open. The outside water height was approximately four feet, but inside we had less than a foot. But we had no option—we went inside and took a rush of water with us. Barb pushed the kayak over to my mother, instructed her to fall back into the solo seat, hoisted the dogs' crate onto my mother's lap, threw the duffel bag of documents at her feet, and started pushing the kayak back onto the street. We pushed into the current, arduously moving the kayak toward the high school. Barb deposited us on a bench outside, glanced up at the sky, wished us luck, and was off.

We never saw Barb again, but we often talk about how we would like to thank her. Barb, with her kayak, was our savior. I hope Barb reads this someday.

At the high school, neighbors gathered around with updates. FEMA still hadn't reached Houston, and no rescues were being made by local emergency crews in our area. We were all stranded. My WhatsApp group was working furiously to find a solution. Finally, around 5:30 PM, an update: my friend's brother-in-law had driven his Hummer as far as he could into our neighborhood, left the vehicle, and brought his personal kayak to assist people who needed to get to higher ground. He was on his way to us. We found out from the neighbors that once you got to the freeway entrance ramp, school buses could take you to a shelter downtown. As my phone battery ran to empty, I relayed this news to my uncle. He lived less than three miles away where it had not flooded, but he could not reach us. The roads were impassable. I told him I would contact him once we could find a functional socket in the high school. For now, we sat, drenched and shaking on the metal benches outside the school, my mother moaning in pain as her medicine wore off.

And then we heard the motor of a boat.

As the metal watercraft came closer, we called out to the three men in bright orange life jackets for help. They swung the boat toward us. They were with FEMA, but they would have to come back for us. A man was potentially having a heart attack in his home farther down the street. They promised they would be back. Hours passed and the skies got darker—this time not from the rain but because night was coming. Around 7:00 PM, the FEMA boat came back and clumsily chucked my mother into the front with her dog at her feet in a crate, alongside an elderly couple they had picked up on the way. I perched on the back with the other dog in my lap, where one of the men was drawing the motor and navigating the back end of the boat.

As we pulled slowly away from the school, a man in a bright yellow kayak yelled out, lengthening my name, "Apaaaaarna. Is that you? I'm Nick. I was told to pick you up!"

Yelling over the motor, I told him we were fine, and he could go on to the next person on his list.

He smiled and waved us onward.

Later, I would learn that Nick rescued a young mother and her newborn next and stayed out paddling around and taking people to the freeway until 2:00 AM. There are truly heroes everywhere you look, especially in times where it's not hell but high waters.

The men taking us to safety told us they were Utah reserve firemen who had driven all night to reach us. They slept for a few hours in cots in a school gym in San Antonio before finally arriving in Houston a few hours prior. Months later, my mother looked up this firehouse and sent a thank-you note, which was received graciously by these selfless reserves.

That night, they dropped us off on the entrance to the freeway. The relief we'd felt from being rescued was slowly being replaced by concern about how we'd survive the shelter. If it were just me, I could manage—but my mom was in chronic pain and our two dogs were terrified.

That's when I saw him. He was standing at the top of the ramp, broad-shouldered and tall.

My uncle—a beacon of light in the most hopeless of moments.

As we huddled together under his umbrella, he explained that he'd been waiting for hours. He came as soon as I texted him from the school. Pure, undiluted relief washed over me as he whisked us away in his car and brought us to his house.

Just a few miles away, life was normal. Roads were not flooded. People were warm and safe in their homes. The bands of rain over Houston were spread out, with some areas being spared and some receiving over fifty inches of rain based on the pattern of the storm. After stripping off our toxic-water clothes and showering, we ate dinner and slipped into bed—my mom, the two dogs, and I—worn out and blissfully safe.

In the morning, I kicked into high gear. We, along with half the city, would need temporary housing. I asked my mom to log into her Realtor account, and within an hour, I rented an apartment for us. It wouldn't be ready for two weeks, but at least we had it lined up.

When the waters receded, the work began.

It wasn't just the massive cleanup of throwing out everything that wasn't salvageable and sorting the rest into boxes—it was also the sudden loss of the life I knew. No one tells you that losing your possessions and your home overnight is accompanied by *all* the stages of grief—at once. I didn't experience each emotion in a neat, orderly sequence. It didn't start with shock and numbness, then move to searching and yearning, before reaching despair and culminating in recovery and reorganization. It was messier. It was all a rush.

It was—fittingly, poetically—a flood of feelings.

There were volunteers to help flood victims organize—well-intentioned friends (and also strangers) who rummaged through your file cabinets and closets and pantry asking you repeatedly, "Throw or keep?" And those volunteers had to be fed three times a day and given popsicles and iced-coffee breaks in the August Houston heat. The volunteers would have to be organized into groups and assigned areas of the house. And with my mom hurt from the rescue and my sister working frantically on her PhD program, I was the first one at the house in the morning and the last one to lock up.

The days were long—and the nights even longer. They were filled with trying to figure out how to file insurance claims, how to furnish a new temporary home, how to find my underwear and clean clothes in the garbage bags of stuff thrown together as "necessary," how to buy two cars when there were none available for hundreds of miles around Houston. They too had flooded in the car lots where they stood.

Life was chaos. And it was in the middle of the chaos that I realized life would never be the same. It could never be restored to pre-flood days. Nine months would pass before we could return to our house. And in those nine months, I had to pivot and maneuver a whole new normal. I also became a survivalist in my own right—focusing on making it through the day, the week, and the months. Never knowing when I would face the next obstacle but always knowing it would be soon. Finding a mattress to sleep on. Negotiating with my workplace to take time off for cleanup. Figuring out how to deal with the severe underpayment from the insurance company. Or just being able to find where the teaspoons were packed. (That last mystery was never solved. New spoons were purchased.)

The loss of my routine, home, possessions—and, most of all, my way of life—led me to an invaluable gain. It allowed me to intimately understand something I hadn't before: that I could lose everything in a heartbeat. That it could happen again.

From that moment on, I began viewing everything material as temporary. As stuff that a random flood could take away from me. That was freeing, cathartic. If I ruined my favorite pair of shoes, dented my car, or lost my sunglasses, it no longer mattered. Stuff did not matter. Stuff wasn't life.

Like I said: boats have shaped who I am.

My time aboard the ship for Semester at Sea had taught me about the world—about our collective strength and resilience. It was the thing that fed my adventurous spirit. My time on the lifeboat during Hurricane Harvey taught me that life was transient. That change was—or could be—certainly around every corner.

And it was all up to me.

Whether from the sameness of a routine or the danger of a hurricane, boats hadn't saved me—*I* had saved me. I had rescued me. And I had changed in the process.

That's what I was doing when I said yes to *Indian Matchmaking*. I was attempting to rescue myself from a life without love. Not because I was unhappy but because I *wanted* love. Just as I wanted to see the world. And to get to safety. I wanted to change my life.

As it turned out, *Indian Matchmaking* was not the boat for that chance at love.

But it was a lifeboat. It did change my life. And me.

2

YOU ARE YOUR
OWN BEST ALLY

S O MANY PEOPLE go through their lives and never work with a
matchmaker. Dare I say, *most* people go through their lives and
never work with a matchmaker. The lucky majority, I call them.
The ones who met in high school or college. The ones who met
at a house party or a bar. The ones who signed up for a website or
swiped right on the perfect match. They never use a matchmaker.
They are gifted the ultimate reward of finding their life partner
without the ineptitude of a meddling force in the process. I am not
one of those people. In fact, I not only used a matchmaker, I also
had the whole experience filmed for the world's viewing pleasure.
So let me explain a matchmaker as best as I can in terms you might
understand. You, after all, might be in that lucky majority.

Consider first people you might have already worked with in
the past: contractors and therapists. And what do contractors and
therapists have in common? They are both service providers: the
former provides materials and labor to renovate a home, while
the latter provides essential mental health counseling. The same
is true of matchmakers. Sima is also in the service industry. She
is not my friend or "aunty" as posited by the title that was flung
upon me by the producers before she entered my door for the

first time. Sima is a professional whose job is to serve her clients' needs by providing them with suitable romantic matches. Or so I naively thought when she was presented to me. And yes, she was presented. That is the word.

It was a balmy Houston day in May when I first met Sima. You might think it was a pivotal moment in my life, but she honestly bears little importance in my entire story of *Indian Matchmaking*. The day I met Sima was the first day of official taping for me.

I had met some of the key members of the crew the day before. They had requested pictures of the inside and outside of my home a few days prior, and their pre-taping visit was to scout the location in person. Their visit was short—a quick tour of the house, an assessment of the driveway width for their equipment van, and a peek at the garage where they would set up their "mission control" the next day. It all checked out. I was nervous, but a showrunner leaned over and gave me a hug when she met me. The crew felt they knew me from my casting tapes, I was told. I was soothed by this fact.

There I was, the night before taping, and any comfort was welcome. I was in an internal tizzy—going over timings of my makeup schedule and my hair appointment before the crew arrived the next day. I was not going to go on a Netflix show with my routine light foundation, cream blush, eyeliner, and dash of lip balm. And I wouldn't let my mother or sister be flailing on the taping day. They would be joining me for the first day, so I made hair and makeup appointments for them too. Were their clothes ready to go? Jewelry? Shoes? I had sorted that out as best as I could. I am always the family stylist, but adding their needs to my own was quite overwhelming.

A physical knot twisted in my stomach as I stood there in my dimly lit living room that evening with these three women producers. I found myself nervously pressing my fingertips to my thumb in repetitive patterns, a mimic of my mind's movements. Over and over, finger by finger, as if I couldn't stop it. The crew left me alone in my home after their brief visit, and I walked it room by room, straightening out the corners of the bedspreads, fluffing out pillows, adjusting artwork so it appeared straighter. I took a deep breath and locked up. I was staying at my mother's house with my pup Conan for the next two nights so that I didn't "mess up" the house for taping. I didn't want to sleep in my perfectly made bed, use the bathtub, or feed Conan in the kitchen where he inevitably created his daily mess. (Conan has no teeth, so feeding him is a process where he drops portions of each bite on the ground if he can't capture it all in his mouth. Welcome to senior rescue dog ownership.) I locked that front door and accepted that I was going to have to let go of what was going to happen next.

We start the first day with my solo visit from Sima. I had not met her before that moment when she knocks on my door while the cameras roll. She was cornered off outside while I was prepped inside for the doorbell ring and the entrance. All I was told prior to meeting her was her name and to call her "Aunty." I sit in my living room waiting for the *ding-dong* of my 1950s bungalow bell. I open the door to a woman in her fifties, blond streaks in her brown hair, a wide nose, and slit eyes that assess me blatantly from the moment they land on me. *It's an Indian aunty thing*, I reason to myself, as I see that skim-over from my hair down to my shoes. *Did she like my dress? Was it the wrong choice? Was the purple and red floral print a bad combination? Did my arms look fat?* "Aunties" care about these details. I am still unclear if this matchmaker "aunty" will too.

What is clear is that is I truly want to find the right partner. I want to get married, maybe even in the next year or two. And this woman was supposed to be the one who would help me. I sit down with Sima—she on the mid-century chair, me on the edge of my gray sectional couch. After initial hellos, she asks me if we can speak in Hindi. I stare blankly at her. I had not expected this request. In my own narrative leading up to this day (you know the one you have in your head that never reflects what actually transpires when the event comes to fruition?), my matchmaker was adept at matchmaking South Asians living in the United States. I imagined her as a woman who was well versed in connecting men and women across this country who could not find each other in the saturated online dating world. I certainly expected to speak in English to my matchmaker. Although I took Hindi for five years in school, I could never quite master the language. Or really, if I'm being honest, I am just terrible at learning other languages. I lived in Italy for six months and left with a vocabulary of forty words. Years later, that Italian roster is likely the six menu items I order at my favorite eateries in Houston.

So when Sima suggests Hindi, I realize that this woman might not understand English well enough to understand my specifications for a partner. But I have no choice to avoid my toddler-level Hindi in discussing this very important subject matter. So I say, "I'd prefer to speak in English. My Hindi is not very good." Sima sighs and we move on to small talk. Where was my family from in India? Oh, I was Sindhi, good, good. Where did my family live currently? Oh, in Mumbai, what neighborhoods? (The right ones, I gathered by her smile at my response.) Do I know xyz? I must, since I said I am related to so-and-so. I want to skip all this chitchat. I am American. I've lived here since I was seven. I want a spouse who understands my background and the way I grew up, someone who understands my educational and career trajectory. I want to tell Sima what I want in a partner, and I need her to listen.

"I want someone more introverted than me," I say first. I consider how to explain further. How do I tell her I want someone who is not an introvert per se but a man more introverted than me? Someone who would tell me it was time to go home at a reasonable time on a night out. Someone who would advocate for a quiet date night at home. It is an easy ask, or so I thought before her understanding of English was in question. How many ways could I articulate these attributes to someone who didn't have a good grasp on my native language? I try once more with the direct line. "Sima Aunty, I'd like someone who is more introverted than me." I am met with silence. "You know, someone who is a wallflower." Or, "Someone who isn't the funniest guy in the room." Maybe I could try, "Someone who doesn't story tell at dinner parties." I veto that one before I say it out loud. The examples slow down when I am met with a blank expression and a slight automatic nod of someone who wants to appear like she's listening. I press on. "I want someone laid-back. Someone who is intelligent—and not just in his career field but in learning about the world around them. And then I'd love for them to share with me." Silence, again. A blank face—expressionless, almost-bored eyes. She finally speaks. "You will be with someone jolly. Someone like you. I have the right man for you." *Jolly?* I look at her in disbelief. Jolly was used exclusively for Santa Claus, and I do not want an elderly man in a red suit. I want the man I had described and, greedily, one who even exceeds those traits I detailed earlier. Instead, I got "jolly."

My mother and sister are brought into the room. They too had been cornered outside in the baking heat, their fresh makeup slowly melting off in the high noon sun. Their hair is curling around their faces, even after tough straightening with heavy products. I am so grateful to see them but also apprehensive. Now the fourteen people squeezed into my living room and camping out in my garage are really here. The two bulky cameras are strapped to the camera people. My mother and sister have microphones attached to their back, and the producers are directing where they should sit. And are they apprehensive? Yes. They weren't going to be comfortable in front of the camera. They are both introverts best suited to small, intimate groups and one-on-one conversations.

But in those moments, when we sit down with Sima for the first time, we still have hope that this will work out. We are presented with two biodatas, "résumés" of potential matches that outline their age, their family background, their careers, and their hobbies. Both men are handsome. But both men are in their forties. I am thirty-four and ready to get married and start a family. These serial bachelors are not what I had in mind.

Sima says, "Just give them a chance." One is Srini, the surfer and mountain lover with his own podcast. The other is Raj, the ER doctor from New York whose hobbies include acting and stand-up comedy. Cue my line to my family, "But you know how I hate comedy." And to clarify, it's true. I tend to not enjoy it unless it's really quality work. I never get through TV shows with a comedic bent. I prefer longer, serialized dramas with a heavy focus on character development. And for stand-up comedy, I'll avoid amateur shows if at all possible. I *will* enjoy (and have many times) the Comedy Cellar in NYC, where famed comedians try out their new material on small crowds. I *will* join friends to see touring comedians, the MVPs who stand in bursting auditoriums with brilliantly rehearsed performances ending with standing ovations. But that quality is not the norm. So normally, I don't like comedy. This was a controversial statement when edited and applied to Srini's jolly status (and not the fact that Raj invested so much of his time in stand-up comedy, per his biodata). But hey,

I stand by it. Some people don't enjoy run-of-the-mill comedic humor. I am one of those people.

So off I go on the dates, amiably giving this matchmaker a chance while knowing full well that none of my criteria was taken into account. But hear me out, here's what I hoped: It wouldn't be bad—I would go on the dates. And who knows? Maybe I would be pleasantly surprised. I was open to the idea that I could easily end up with a man I had never seen myself with on paper. I was not thrilled, but I was open. Since you've likely watched the show, we all know how Srini went. *Poorly* is a generous summary, but we will get into that whole saga. I promise—just hold tight for now.

Months later, watching the show for the first time, I was shocked to hear Sima call me negative and unbalanced after our first meeting. So . . . *not* jolly? Apparently not. The early episodes continue to show Sima depicting me in a negative light behind my back in solo interviews on the screen, which honestly puzzles me to no end. And even worse? She called my mother negative too. Why? To this day, I will never understand what made that woman say such horrible things about me. She was in my house all day, eating her meals at my dining room table after we taped. Her husband, daughter, and assistant were on set and were given seats at my table too. I invited these guests into my house and then later, on screen, saw her slamming me for my negativity.

Tangentially, in a surprising turn of events, I did love the taping process when it was happening in real time. I found it so interesting to see a whole new world unfold in my own living room, kitchen, and dining room on those days. I did. Sure, it was draining and the days were long. Sure, I was disappointed every time a date didn't work out. But this world was so fascinating, and the people in it were so new to me. They had unique career trajectories that had led them to this very job, and they lived so far outside my reality of a stiff, corporate world filled with toxic lawyers and brutal office politics. They made *things*—in this world, they made what we consumed, and I was in awe of the whole process. I was swept up in the bright and shiny world of entertainment. And in so many ways, I could sit back and observe it. There were fourteen of them, and they traveled together to all the other contributors, unknown to me by name or location during taping. I was the outsider, and as they got more comfortable with me and my home, they started to forget I was there. It was the best part. I loved hosting this clan of mismatched creatives, each one so hilarious in their own right.

I have clear memories of sitting outside at picnic tables in my front yard, eating loud and casual lunches with the crew and producers; of the time I bought them all Indian chai and samosas from my favorite hole-in-the-wall; of the mochi ice cream I passed around in my garage, a.k.a. "mission control"; of them singing Lizzo lyrics loudly throughout my house while setting up the next scene; of them comforting me when I was tired or defeated.

I look back on it now and remember the amazing individuals who made up the crew: the kind but zinger-filled cameraman who had married his high school sweetheart, the musically talented sound guy who always put a sponge behind the microphone on my back because it left bruises by the end of the day, the cheery but brusque line producer from Atlanta, the eager production assistants, the second cameraman patiently learning from his senior mentor. They were just doing their job. They were just trying to get in and out of Houston and get back to their families. But in the meantime, they were also creating magic for the screens of people around the world. It was, in the literal sense, awe-some.

In its own right, my press journey was a different kind of awe-some, more drawn out but all starting with the *New Yorker* magazine. It was my first interview, and it was at 9:00 AM on July 16, 2019—seven hours after the show was released to the general public. The show came out on July 16, 2019, at 12:00 AM PT, which is 2 AM CT. Shekar and I sat on our phones—he in Chicago and me in Houston—pressing refresh on our remotes until *Indian Matchmaking* appeared. We nervously both hung up to watch our own portions before going to bed. I had been forewarned on the phone a few days prior that my mother "might not like her story arc" but had no other indication of what was to come. All I knew was I had to watch every part I was in before I joined Smriti and Sima for the *New Yorker* interview. I watched all my episodes by myself, curled up on the sofa hugging my churning stomach and shaking in shock by the end of episode five. Who was this angry, bitter woman on my screen? Why was my mother being shown as an overbearing witch? Why were there flat-out omissions that changed my story line completely? I went to bed that night uncertain of what I had just seen. I comforted myself as I rocked myself to sleep at 5:30 AM.

I am up at 8:00 AM for a work call, because yes, I didn't take the day off from my full-time job as an attorney. By 9:00 AM, I am on a Zoom call with Smriti and Sima and the journalist from the *New Yorker*. She asks benign questions, seemingly most interested in her angle on Sima, and moves on with the interview quickly. This is the first and last time I speak to Sima after the show launch. It consists of a few pleasantries and a lukewarm congratulations on the show. She had, after all, called me negative and stubborn—and, to add insult to injury, included my mother in her derogatory confessionals.

Press goes on for days upon days. I watch this first-season show quickly become viral. Along with its virality comes the lashing out against my portrayal. Yet I don't correct the falsehoods when speaking to the journalists filling up my calendars in those first days. I know I have to hire a publicist to deal with the vitriol on the internet. After many introductory phone calls, I found it would cost me $10,000 to $15,000 for a three-month retainer. There is no way I can afford it.

My friend in Los Angeles chuckles when I tell her what's happening to me behind the scenes of this successful show launch. I am a babbling mess of tears before she calms me down. "It's called show business, Aparna. Business. The business of making a great show. And *this* is a great show." This lawyer from Houston had some lessons to learn, apparently.

Simultaneously with all my press interviews—because believe me, everything is happening at once in the days after the show launch—my sister mentions to me that Sima called me "mentally unbalanced." Now, my sister isn't a lawyer, but she makes a good point. Should Sima be allowed to publicly state a medical opinion with no credentials to support it? Incensed, and with renewed hope that I could have a third-party confirm my hurt feelings from Sima's words are based on actionable wrongs, I frantically begin reaching out to friends on the West Coast, polling each one for their connections to top entertainment lawyers in L.A. A former coworker in Houston swoops in with a lead. His friend from Jewish summer camp as a teen was an entertainment lawyer at a firm in Los Angeles before recently moving to Minnesota with her baby. This tenuous connection got me a phone call with a top attorney whose photo online showed him to be a debonair, silver-haired man in his mid-to-late fifties. His client list was impressive. However, on our phone call, I was told I had no case. This attorney had lost multimillion-dollar cases on a lot more compelling facts. I am deflated, yes, but honestly, I knew I would never bring a claim against anyone in court anyway. I was sad, mad, and every emotion in between. But not ever going to take it further.

At a certain point, I realize I have hit a proverbial wall. It appears the world has chosen to hate me based on a television show. But I have my own choices to make, and I choose to stand in my own truth regardless. As journalists reach out from every corner of the globe, I choose to speak up and tell my own story. At around week three of the post-launch hysteria, I begin tentatively telling those reporters who ask specifically about my mother's choice words to call Srini a "loser" that they were based on things the viewer didn't see, off camera. By week four, I am more brazen and even begin to describe my own feelings about my off-camera portion of the evening with Srini—how I was hurt, disrespected, and understandably upset. While never revealing the specifics, I remind reporters that any woman who is treated this way *should* declare she "will speak to that man never." And the most amazing twist I hadn't anticipated? Whether by coincidence or just by nature of the field, almost every reporter I encounter is a woman. And every woman is both enraged and empathetic. I feel victorious. The trolls quiet down, and the press is pouring in with support for me. While I started as just a "lawyer in Houston," I feel I have successfully turned the tides by myself.

I am left with an empowering epiphany about perseverance, about grit, and about belief in self. For all the women who have been dismissed as crazy, unstable, negative, or stubborn—or for any woman who has cried or screamed in expressing frustration for feeling unseen or unheard or dismissed—this is my declaration to them: Don't let them silence you with their name calling. You are not "negative" or "unbalanced." Nor are you "stubborn" or "demanding." Don't let them turn your life into a playground where they are the bullies and you are the victim. Speak up. And don't give up. I was an advocate for myself when no one would stand up for me. I was my own best ally. And every woman can do the same for herself, whether her stage is small and familial or she's flung into a worldwide theater. The power is hers alone. And I took back my power.

3

DON'T WASTE TIME
ON LOSERS

PROMISED THIS DEEP DIVE EARLIER, so it seems fitting we take the plunge into the real story behind the Mom-proclaimed "loser" now.

The camera lights shine brightly into my eyes as I settle on the edge of the gray sectional couch in my living room. I am cold, even though it is a balmy day. My mother, sister, and brother-in-law are on the couch. Sima is seated on one of the chairs, with one left empty for Srini. My mom is taking on the brunt of this strained interaction by making small talk with Sima, while I smile nervously and try to subdue the knots in my stomach.

It feels like it has taken lifetimes to get to this moment when I meet my first proposed match by Sima. I am still convinced that one of these two men on the papers she presented can be my future husband. I want badly to believe in the power of a matchmaker—this omnipotent, ever powerful love seeker for the singles of the world who were wandering around hoping to find their match at a wedding, at the grocery store, or through a friend.

She would pull the perfect man out of a hat for me. I contrived her into a magician before I even met her. I am less certain now after our one-on-one chats when she declared I needed someone jolly, but I am going to give it a try anyway. This is no time to be petulant and turn away these matches who were allegedly chosen by the famed Sima herself. To be honest, had I seen either of these men on a dating app, I would have swiped left. But then, I reason, maybe that's why I'm still single.

I rack my brain to recall Srini's biodata, tugging down my heavy knit shirt and hoping the high-waisted jeans adequately flatten any unintended tummy bulges. Perpetually nervous about unseemly camera angles, I am particularly uncomfortable in this outfit.

My original plan was to wear a sunny yellow silk dress, but the field producer informed me that would only work if I wore closed-toe shoes. My date with Srini was an activity that she could not tell me about but that had strict rules about closed-toe shoes. That dress didn't go with pumps. So I rushed to my closet room and frantically searched for an alternative that wasn't already lined up with the perfect accessories. I was not happy with this "surprise" turn of events. I surveyed my armoires, one by one. Nothing. It had to be solid prints or not be "too busy" to film well. It had to be an outfit I could be active in, without knowing what the activity was, of course. I went back out to the living room to run a few options by the producers and cameraman, while also pressuring them for more information on where we were going. Almost to the end of the hallway, I stopped to hear them discussing ax throwing. *Aha.* I was going ax throwing. Wait, *ew.* I was going ax throwing. I went back to the closet room without letting them know I had heard my intended destination. The new mint green top was selected, along with high-waisted jeans. That would work when I lifted my hands above my head to fling the ax toward the target. Patent blush wedges would allow me to take the steps forward with ax in hand. I was set.

So here I am, boxy knit top that is too short for comfort, waiting for the doorbell to ring once again—this time with Sima inside and a newcomer, my first date, outside. I brace myself and am given the cue that we are rolling. I rise to open the door for him. Sima joins me as the cohostess. He's smiling when I open the door, and I immediately relax. This will be fine. He's amiable enough—I could tell that from his biodata. He could do this, and so could I. I give him a quick introductory hug and show him to his chair. A nondescript but "jolly" conversation follows in which he shares that he skydives, that he once lived in Texas as a child, and that he not only has his own podcast but also does motivational speaking. I am relieved to see he is affable enough to carry a conversation with a roomful of strangers while in front of two cameras and a film crew. We wrap that scene within an hour, and Sima exits with my family. Srini and I are left to chat with each other as the crew is outside outfitting my hybrid Lexus sedan with an inside camera to capture my drive to the date with Srini in my passenger seat.

We take a bottle of wine—the place we are going is BYOB, apparently. (Don't get me started on whether ax-throwing locations should have a bring-your-own-booze policy.) I am not letting on that I know where we are going, so I grab a Cabernet and search for my wine opener to take along. Not able to find my usual one, I pull out my grandfather's stainless-steel German wine opener from his visit to Frankfurt in the 1970s. Within thirty minutes, we are situated in my car. I put down my window from the driver's seat, and I'm told our destination. I feign surprise with nervous laughs, and the producer is properly pleased with their decision to send me ax throwing.

The drive is relatively painless, small talk with a side of awk-wardness at the camera set up in the middle of the dashboard. We arrive at the strip mall to find the crew needs thirty minutes to set up the lighting and cameras. Smriti accompanies Srini and I to a Thai restaurant, jesting that she is chaperoning us to make sure we save "all the good stuff" for our date. Srini orders a glass of wine, so I do the same. I'm not a huge drinker, but I realize downing a glass of wine can't possibly do anything but help. Our liability waivers for ax throwing are executed at the table. They're rushed upstairs, and we are left to chat about my time living in the "real South," Nashville, while in law school. We joke about southern culture that allows you to say nasty things about people with the caveat that you add, "Bless their heart" after. He's laughing, and I know we can make it through this date.

We are led to the second story of the strip mall and enter the ax-throwing place to applause from a laughing crowd. They're cheering as we are walked in toward the back corner. I'm blushing, thankfully not noticeable under my brown skin and heavy stage blush applied earlier by the makeup artist.

The owners lead us to the far back target and explain the rules and technique to us. We are given red plastic cups and told we could open our wine whenever we are ready. Um, ready? But first, we have to attempt the actual ax throwing. Srini goes first, taking a powerful step forward and flinging the ax against the target. It falls to the ground without catching the wood wall. He hands me the ax. In my stiff shirt, I can't lift my arms all the way up. I clearly can't tell anyone that, so I do my best to throw the heavy ax toward the wall. I watch groups of friends next to me—laughing, drinking beers, taking turns one by one to pause their chatter for a moment to attempt the throwing of an ax. They are dressed comfortably, no awkward mic on their back, carefree and enjoying the company they keep. I have bright lights on me, a shirt I can barely move in, heavy makeup on my face, and only Srini and a film crew for company. I sigh. *What did I sign myself up for?* With an envious look back, I take the ax handed to me. I try five times in row, missing each time. The cameraman focuses on me with arm outstretched, following the ax as it hits the wall and falls flat on the floor. This happens over and over. I am so frustrated. The wine is opened and I take gulps, wishing away this situation. At one point, the wine misses my mouth and falls straight down my shirt. On camera. I rush to the restroom, and thankfully the same thick knit I have come to hate apparently doesn't soak in liquids. Its nonporous outer layer allows the wine to roll off, and any residual stain is minimal. I stare at myself in that white neon light of the bathroom, wondering why my cheeks are so flushed and how I can fix my unruly hair. I can't. And I have to go back outside. I am told to try one more time with the ax when I return to our station. After being assured that the red wine had not stained my shirt, I pick up the ax. I nail it, straight on the target. Even the cameraman smiles. It is so fitting. Our ax throwing is complete, but not our date.

The production assistants pull up two stools situated so Srini and I are in the same frame. The chitchat is short. I inquire about his job, trying to figure out what he actually does each day. I only know my own office work in a legal corporate America, and I am genuinely curious about what a workday looks like for someone with a nontraditional career. Our on-camera date comes to a close with me suggesting we grab a bite to eat.

I had decided I would take him to dinner, since it was 10:00 PM and we hadn't eaten yet. For me, it seemed fair to start a practice of taking each date out after taping was done to give him a chance to be himself—no microphone, no lights, no crew. I would start with Srini.

As we close our taping with three takes of our formal "exit" from the ax-throwing location, I am hit with an overwhelming exhaustion. Day two is officially over. I have one more date the next day with a kickoff 7:00 AM hair and makeup appointment. I brace myself for dinner with Srini, noting that most kitchens will be closed. A bar will have to do. One of the producers kindly reminds me that I don't have to take him out, but I insist that it is proper etiquette considering his effort to come out here. And besides, he is innocuous enough—I still pressured myself into keeping an open mind, knowing full well that his gregarious, evasive on details, thrill-seeking ways are likely not a fit for me. Had we met on a dating app, I would have ended the date with a quick hug and no follow-up. But these are different circumstances. We wave goodbye to the production team and head down the stairs to my car.

First stop: a greenhouse bar, its outdoor chandeliers welcoming us in. With only a few menu items offered at this late hour, Srini asks if we can go to a proper sit-down restaurant. I don't want to drop him off hungry, so I drive to a delicious modern American restaurant with a kitchen close time of 11:00 PM. We make it just in time and are invited to order right away. He orders another drink while I stick to water. After the wine drinking that started at the Thai restaurant and followed through the taped portion, I am sleepy, discombobulated, and ready to hydrate for my long day tomorrow.

He pushes me to tell him about my next day over our meal. It's finally my chance to be evasive. It's not my style to not be direct and just state that I have hair and makeup tomorrow morning and then another date. I am, after all, a participant on a dating show, so I am not sure where the surprise would be if I mentioned I had another date, but I avoid his question. He continues on, declaring that he's "so proud of us for doing such a great job for the cameras." I narrow my eyes. Excuse me? For the cameras? Was he kidding? I assess his face. No, he is serious. "Didn't we do great for them? I think they liked our banter. Its obvious we are both great on camera." I direct a wan smile at him, but a wave of disappointment washes over me. Am I the only one taking this opportunity to find a partner seriously? I do not have the energy to dissect this vein of thought.

Weariness from the two long days of taping with another looming in a matter of hours makes me bite my tongue. Dinner winds down, he politely offers to pick up the check, and we leave in my car.

I pull up to his hotel's circle driveway hoping for a quick escape. No such luck. Unbuckling his seatbelt, Srini turns to me for what becomes a long-winded diatribe on his play-by-play experience through casting and meeting Sima earlier that day. My eyes glaze over as I listen to him speak, his eyes bloodshot and his words flowing quickly.

I watch the clock in the car go from 1:30 AM to 2:30 AM and then near 3:00 AM. I have to be up in four hours. I'm jolted out of internal gymnastics when I hear him say, "I mean, you're cute and all, but what did they think sending me to Houston, Texas? Why would I date someone who lives here when I am in San Diego?" I look at him incredulously. "What do you mean? They thought we would do long distance to get to know each other. You know, planes, trains, cars . . . FaceTime." He scoffs at me. "Yea, right. I would never date someone long-distance. My last relationship was a girl in Chicago and she lied to me so badly. I'm still reeling from that and it was years ago." I reason with him, still not processing fully what he was saying. "Well, it sounds like she was untruthful and that had nothing to do with distance. Those two things aren't correlated." He retorts, "Maybe not, but I would never date you. But good luck! I'm sure you'll do great. You have my number, so

text me as this goes on. I want to hear how everything turns out."
I am speechless, which is rare but now becoming increasingly
common with this one man. I am in shock at his intent to never
date me but his apparent need to still come and waste everyone's
time in Houston. Not only the production team's but also my
family's and my time. This is too much.

Here I am, genuinely (and naively) taking this process to heart,
and he is slapping me on the shoulder with a friendly laugh,
mocking me for considering any sort of future for us. I have to
ask, and so I do. "So why did you come?" And his response is
"Well, they called me yesterday, and I thought it would be fun. I
was very clear with them, though. I would not ever date someone
who didn't live in San Diego or Los Angeles." Disgusted with him
and needing him to get out of my car, I say, "It was certainly quite
the experience. I better go now. I have an early start tomorrow."
I take the car out of Park purposefully and stare at him until he
opens the door and exits. I expect to be livid, but instead I am
just numb on my drive home. I pull into my mother's driveway
where I am staying that night and lean onto the steering wheel,
draping myself over the top as I cry hearty tears of exhaustion
and defeat. All of that—the hair, the makeup, the clothes, the date,
the "polite" after-date dinner—all for nothing. This man had no
intent of ever giving me a chance.

I sleep fitfully, wake up with dark circles under my eyes, and
ask my sweet makeup artist to please cover it all up. We have one
more day of taping, and I want to make it go as smoothly as possible. I don my yellow silk sundress, originally intended for Srini,
and head to the cooking class across town. Some producers assure
me today's date will be much better. I roll my eyes. "That won't be
hard." And then it dawns on me; Srini still has my grandfather's
vintage steel wine opener that he bought in Germany so many
years ago. He had slipped it into his pocket as we exited the

ax-throwing venue. I want it back. A producer steps up and says she will text him and get it back for me. Losing my dignity was one thing; losing the sentimental wine opener was another. (Side note: I never got the wine opener back.)

My date with Raj is an easy day. He is shy but kind. Noncommittal but easy to be around. He certainly did not want to date anyone long-distance either—that he made abundantly clear. After macaron-making, we head back to my home where we film an awkward forty-five-minute chat in my backyard. We wrap the date, and Raj is off. As I lead him through the house, I hear loud voices outside the front door. It's my mother, and the first thing I notice is her flushed face and the vein popping in her neck. She is angry.

I'm alarmed to see her speaking to producers in raised tones. Sima is in the garage, lurking close enough to catch drifts of the conversation until an assistant removes her from that vantage spot. I keep an eye on the situation as I take Raj toward the waiting car. He's also peering over my shoulder, telling me I shouldn't worry about him and should instead take care of . . . that. "Good luck," he wishes me as he steps in the vehicle. I never see or hear from Raj again. But that's the last thing on my mind at that moment. I head over to the spectacle unleashed on my front yard.

"Mom, what's going on? Is everything OK here?" The producers are looking frazzled, trying to calm down my mother. My sister is clearly agitated as well. She's about to fill me in, as I hear my mother continuing her questioning. "What is this show? What is this about? Is it you trying to make my daughter look bad? Is it you trying to create drama?" Smriti is resigned from her repeated attempts to assure my mother that this is no such show. "This is a docuseries that's highlighting the best parts of our culture, Aunty. That was always my intent. Maybe this was a miscommunication with Sima Didi?" (*Didi* is a respectful term for *sister*, and Smriti uses it liberally when referring to Sima.) My mom spits back, "She said it in Hindi. There was no miscommunication. I understood her perfectly well." I step into the small circle. "What happened here? Smriti?" My mother glares at her while Smriti stumbles over her words, trying carefully to not further ruffle feathers. I glance toward the garage. Sima has been seated on a folding chair. She sits there defiantly staring in our direction, arms crossed. Smriti explains, "It appears your mother and Sima have had a misunderstanding." My mother's vein throbs behind her ear and down her neck. "Again, I understood her fine. I will not have that woman speak about my daughter like that. How are we supposed to trust she will find a match for my daughter when she clearly thinks so poorly of her?"

I raise one eyebrow. I am at my wits' end. What now? It's the end of the three days, this crew will be gone tomorrow morning, and I have negative deposits of energy at this point. I know this doesn't have anything to do with Srini. I got to my mother's house at 3:00 AM the night prior and left at 7:00 AM before she woke up to go to my makeup appointment. I rack my brain for context as Smriti ushers us into the house and into my closet room. My mother spews the whole story to me the moment she and my sister close the door behind us. Smriti stays in the room as my mother tells me that Sima had pulled her aside yesterday as they left my house and as Srini and I prepared to depart for the ax-throwing portion of our day.

According to my sister, Sima first pulled my sister and my brother-in-law Darrin to the side outside and asked to chat. Sima relayed to them that I have to be told to "have less opinions." My brother-in-law took a sharp inhale and raised his eyebrows at Sima, as Sima quickly backpedaled to add, "or Aparna should stop saying her opinions so strongly. You should talk to her." Darrin immediately responded, "But that's not who she is. Why should she change that? It wouldn't be fair to her or the guy ultimately.

Why would we ever encourage her to do that?" Sima is aghast that he wouldn't agree to do her bidding. My sister stepped in. "If you say she's opinionated, then that is who she is. That's how I am too. And that will be the very reason someone chooses to marry her. If she has to hide who she really is, what kind of marriage would that be?"

My mother interjects that she heard the tail end of this conversation when she walked toward the three of them the day before. Darrin walked away, frustrated. Vansa followed, and Mom looked at Sima questioningly. According to my mother, Sima then said to her in Hindi, "Srini is a very nice boy, and your daughter will only agree that he's so nice if you convince her. These matches are good ones. You need to make her understand." My mother, shocked by these pointed statements, quickly retorted, "Why would I want to convince my daughter to be with someone? She should choose with her own free will to be with someone." Sima responded, "Your daughter is very powerful. You need to tone her down. This will not do for the men I am bringing to her." That was enough for my mother. "How dare you? My daughter is powerful because I have brought her up to be powerful. She will choose her own partner. It is not for me to decide who she will marry." Sima, seeing this disregard for her advice, left the conversation clucking and saying, "OK. It's up to you. We will see how this goes."

I stand in that room, the color draining from my face. The woman I entrusted with finding my perfect match not only sent me wholly unsuitable matches but also spoke so poorly of me directly to my family. Still trying to keep the peace so that my mom's anger doesn't shut down the whole show at this moment, I ask Smriti the meaning of such statements. Smriti makes pithy excuses for what is clearly Sima's poor etiquette coupled with archaic views of matchmaking.

I don't want to add fuel to the fire, but I have to make my mother and sister aware of the Srini situation—his inappropriate comments, for starters, and the absolute dismissal of me for living in Houston, even though he agreed to get on a plane and meet me. I stop the conversation, relay my date, and see my mom's neck turn blotchy red from anger. She turns her steely gaze to Smriti. "This is who Sima set my daughter up with? This is who she wants me to convince my daughter to be with? Is this a joke?" Smriti again placates her and asks us if we would share these concerns with Sima on camera. We agree but ask for a few minutes to calm down before we return to the living room.

With Smriti gone, my mother turns to me. "You can leave right now. You don't owe these people anything. If Sima keeps matching you with these perennial bachelors in their forties who have no intention of settling down, what are you even doing here? And you said you were crying last night when you got home. I don't want that for you. You shouldn't want that for yourself, darling." She's right. I know she is. But I am not ready to give up on the notion that this could work out for me. That this process could leave me with my future partner.

In the living room, Sima is already seated on the chair. My mother, sister, and I file out and take our seats on the couch and the chair beside her. The cameras start rolling. I lay out my grievances, mostly focusing on that fact that Sima has to vet the men she's presenting to me better. She has to make sure they're serious about finding a relationship, that they're in the right mind-set to consider getting married if they find the right person, and that they understand any relationship with me would start long-distance. My mother jumps in and explains that I am willing to put in the work of making a long-distance relationship work, if I like the person. I need matches that better align with where I am in life. Sima shrugs and exclaims again that these were good matches.

My mother gets more irritated, muttering as you all heard on television, "Srini, the Loser." To her, any man that makes me cry, any man that disrespects my time, any man that uses this opportunity for publicity for himself, is a loser. I don't disagree. And I know I need to stay far away from any Mom-defined losers.

The lights dim and the cameras stop rolling. The tiredness aches from my eyes to my neck down my body to the heels strapped around my ankles. It's over. I want these people out of my house. In their defense, they knew I was done with them. They were kind enough to apologize for my horrible experiences and explain they never intended for it to be such a negative first filming. I forgive them, knowing full well that while they may have made mistakes, they're good people and had the best of intentions. They were on my team, and they also wanted me to find love.

In hindsight, I was still treading carefully because I didn't want to upset *them*, fearing they wouldn't give me any more matches because I was too "difficult." In that desperation, I sacrificed my own dignity and ignored my intuition to stick up for myself—or even to walk away completely.

It is not until the cameras return a second time that I state clearly that I do not stand for people disrespecting me or my family. Srini had texted me the day after our taping to wish me luck with the process, and I refused to answer, even to ask for my grandfather's wine opener. Because here's the thing: disrespect me once, and I will cut you out of my life completely. My now famed words, "I will talk to you never" was stated matter-of-factly in that on-camera interview.

Fast-forward a year and a half later, and I am watching the show at 2:00 AM when it drops on Netflix. I inhale deeply when the first episode opens with Srini. When my mother mutters, "Srini, the Loser," I am stunned. I realize the viewer thinks my family and I don't like Srini because, as a podcaster, he is not successful enough for me. All the viewer sees is me announcing I will "talk to you never." My mother calling Srini a loser for what appears to be his job triggers all-out hatred from trolls and average viewers alike. It strikes me then that the fact that I didn't stand up for myself during the filming of the show, fearing that voicing my displeasure would be accompanied by consequences, namely not being set up with men moving forward, resulted in viewers hurling hateful words at a haughty, elitist woman with no regard for a man with a creative career path. From my point of view, I was the one who was walked all over. I was the one who was treated poorly by Srini. I was the one who was left crying in my car after a defeating date.

Yet, from how I see it, the world around me is viewing my portrayal on the show as a full insight into who I am as a person when I do not personally identify with the Aparna on screen at all. My friends are sending me any positive DMs they can find, but one finally breaks down with some bad news. Eva Chen—*the* Eva Chen, with her 1.2 million followers—posts about *Indian Matchmaking* in her stories. She actually posts about me, bashing me outright and standing up for Srini. She goes as far as to link his podcast with a "Swipe Up," telling her followers to give his incredible podcast a listen. I'm stunned. I stare at the story post, my finger on my screen, letting her words burn my eyes. I admire this woman so much—or I did. A former fashion editor and now the head of fashion at Instagram, I had idolized her for her unique career trajectory, as well as her flawless style. And here she is, bad-mouthing me to her huge Instagram following. Srini was not cut from the show, or even downplayed. No, instead Srini was given the fame he came to get initially. I am hurt—oh so hurt—but also reeling from Eva Chen's flippant dismissal of me. She's in the industry, to a certain extent. She's at least in the limelight. If she can't grasp that reality TV is likely not the *real-life* truth, how could the average viewer on their couch? That I am not just some woman who is unworthy of love.

It hits me like a ton of bricks. Maybe *I* consumed reality television without discerning it as only pure entertainment in the past. Not one to watch much television currently, I think back to my twenties when I religiously followed *The Bachelor* franchise. Did I take the version presented to me on screen as truth then? Did I believe a certain woman was a villain based on her story line? I am racked with guilt, even without being able to pinpoint if I had committed myself to these judgments in the past. I now realize that people seen on screen are likely manipulated and contorted into convenient arcs created by story producers. And that in fact, our judgments of them as human beings—as complex and nuanced individuals with their own backstory—are completely skewed by two-dimensional portrayals.

I want to believe we as a society can do better than these contrived understandings of the media we consume. *The Bachelor* franchise debuted over twenty-five years ago, and yet here we are believing everything we are fed on our televisions. Aren't we wiser to these tropes? Don't we yet realize that women can be all of it—strong and vulnerable, confident and introspective, conquerors and empaths? Can't we see that women are complex yet filled with grace as they navigate a world that doesn't always hold a space for them? Aren't we better than those who cast harsh assessments of the vilified strong women on their social media platforms without a second thought? I sure hope so, and if we are not there as a society now, I plead that we all get there soon.

4

THEY TOLD ME I WAS GOING TO DIE ALONE. I WAS WAITING FOR THEM TO CALL ME UGLY.

IT WAS JULY 16, 2020, forever now known as "launch day" in my life. The followers streamed in on my Instagram account. *Ping, ping, ping.* Comments on photos dating back two or more years lit up my notifications. And my DMs were full—hundreds of messages already sitting there, unopened. I sat down to respond to them around 9:00 PM and then, I saw it. Someone, a stranger—also known as a troll—had commented on my most recent grid post. (*Grid post* versus *story* was not lingo I was well versed in at the time, but now I use it freely and frequently.) Anyway, yes, a troll. And he (or she?) decided to make a crude comment about how I deserved to die alone. I was shocked. Standing in my kitchen, headed to the couch to sit down and plunge into the social media frenzy, I was stunned. I looked around my home, as if someone could see my shame and embarrassment. Silence. So I looked for the delete button, swiped the comment quickly into a virtual Instagram trashcan, and breathed a sigh of relief. Whew, that was a close call. But I had caught it just in time. The troll had posted it only minutes prior to me seeing it. I skimmed through the direct messages, all of them from fans loving the show and wondering how they had all finished it within twenty-four hours of it airing. Who were these people? And how did they find this show? There was no hype, no billboard in Times Square, no press frenzy around this show. This was some first-season docuseries about the failed relationships of seven South Asians and one traditional match-maker. The whole situation struck me as bizarre.

I went to bed, sleeping fitfully for a few hours before waking up at 7:00 AM for another interview. Press had already started, and I naively assumed it would be a busy two weeks of promot-ing the show. I had already had my first few interviews. Mind you, the very first was the *New Yorker* magazine, which I was fascinated by—because again, to me, this show was just . . . so unknown. On those first days after its launch, we didn't know the grand scale of what this show would one day be. And along that grand scale of nonstop domestic and international press came nonstop domestic and international trolls. The morning of July 17, I opened Instagram to find an angry slew of comments that pointed out I was deleting comments. First of all, I had only deleted one, not the many these comments called me out for. Second, who were these crazy people? And why did they care so much? Why also were they so cruel? Long, scathing attacks on my character, my family, my home decor, and even my adopted rescue dogs came rushing in like a tidal wave of hatred. And this was just one platform. It did not start or stop there.

Smriti, the creator and executive producer of the show, had told me on our phone call the week prior to the launch that she was most looking forward to "building an Aparna hive" on Twitter. I enthusiastically agreed that it would be fun to engage in dis-course about the show and our matchmaking practices in India and within its diaspora communities. Mind you, I hadn't seen the show yet, so I wasn't quite sure why there would be so much anticipated conversation. But in my people-pleasing way, I shared in Smriti's excitement and announced I would start a Twitter account just to play a role in these dialogues with viewers of the show. I created the account on July 10. The show launched on July 16. On July 19, I deactivated my Twitter account completely. In those three days, all I saw was notification after notification alerting me to a hate storm swirling around my name: abusive, hurtful tweets, deep-rooted in misogyny and sexism—most of them from men. I struggled with reading each one but forced myself to continue "seeing what was out there." I was distraught. I was physically ill within two days. My mother and sister were watching me walk around them in a daze, constantly attached to my phone, wavering between anger for the hate being spewed at me, fear of never meeting a South Asian man who would accept me after this show, and downright defeat that I got myself into a situation so naively and with so much optimism, never once imagining *this* to be my new reality.

So my family sat me down to eat dinner on July 19, physically pushing me to the table and telling me to put away my phone. I was hardly eating, not drinking water, barely sleeping more than a few hours a night, and my mood swings were fierce and sudden—crying, furious, sad, tired, defeated, betrayed, overwhelmed. Rinse and repeat. Over and over. My mother brought it up over hot aloo parathas and sweet achar. "Maybe you should just quit Twitter." I sat with it for a second. Quit? Wait, was that possible? I asked my sister. She didn't agree. In her academic world, Twitter was the number one forum for spirited conversations and healthy debate. Didn't I want to participate in it? No, I didn't. I wanted to quit. I grabbed my phone from the console behind me, googled how to deactivate a Twitter account, went to the app, and deleted my presence in that world. In that moment, for just that one moment, I felt powerful. I felt in control. And I suddenly felt voraciously hungry. I ripped off a large piece of the paratha on my plate and dunked it in cold yogurt before stuffing it in my mouth. I finished one and then grabbed for another. I was eating as if I had run a marathon. My family beamed at each other. This was one right move. This was boundary setting. And most important, this is my life, and it is my right to weed out negativity. There would be no hive. There would be no more vitriol—at least on that one platform.

And it turns out that Facebook isn't any different than Twitter. Any public post celebrating my positive press is littered with hateful comments from men and sometimes even women. By sharing those articles on Facebook, I was trying to show my own small Universe that there was some good left in me, even after that edit ripped me to shreds and left me as a cold, elitist bitch. But then the trolls found me there too. I posted the articles in "public" mode, forgetting that keyboard warriors can (and will) find you anywhere on the internet. Right after the empowerment I felt from my Twitter deactivation, I decided to implement some boundaries for my Facebook world. Since I am an old-time user of the platform, dating back to 2005, I was uncomfortable with the idea of cutting myself off from my personal network grown thoughtfully over the past fifteen years. A lot of my "friends" on Facebook are older relatives, parents of my friends, or coworkers who are on no other platform. While simply deleting my Facebook account was an option, I remained stubborn and principled that *Indian Matchmaking* would not take away what was already mine before the show entered my life. Sweet messages from great uncles, birthday wishes from my best friend's grandmother, and archived photos from old teachers from grade school would not cease because this show decided to craft its own version of the truth.

My compromise was that I kept my Facebook more private than Instagram. I declined the multitude of friend requests filling my inbox and accepted only those people with whom I have more than five mutual friends. While an arbitrary rule, it made decision-making for each request much easier for me in those days when decisions had to be made practically every second. I left the press article posts public but edited many older posts to make them accessible only to connected friends on the platform. As for those trolls who appeared relentlessly to bash me in the comments section of my CNN, *Vulture*, and *Oprah* magazine articles? Well, I liberally blocked those individuals and deleted their comments. I find this strategy works on Facebook exclusively.

Mean notes still came pouring into a folder for messages from people who are not my friends on Facebook. I read each one. Each one crushed me a little more. But I didn't respond. I just deleted. Until one day, when a man sent me a Facebook message with a picture of himself shirtless. He's overweight, of South Asian descent, and is lounging like a beached whale on a printed, grungy sofa. He is holding a gun in his hand and his eyes glint with lewd innuendo. His message says, "Hi Aparna. How was Srini?? He likes you very much . . . he likes you very much in an orange dress."

I saw this message and my heart started beating uncontrollably, thumping in my chest and banging into my ribs. I was scared. Flat out petrified. Just that morning, someone I didn't know had tagged me in an Instagram story. I opened it and saw a picture of my house. He had parked right outside my front door and was posting pictures of my house on his Instagram story. This man had looked up my home on public records, gotten in his car, parked at my house, taken photographs of my front door, and asked his followers, "Think this bitch is home?" I used to casually go out the front door in pajamas to pick up errant UPS and FedEx packages thrown toward the house by mail delivery drivers. My pup would follow me to sniff around and mark a few of his favorite spots. It was our routine. And now I was scared. Who else was going to be in front of my house? I had to google again. I was learning all my new life tricks from Google. How to deactivate Twitter. How to take your name off public records. A host of search queries I wouldn't wish on my enemies.

So when this picture came in, gun-toting nudity with slit eyes that seemed to look straight through my phone at me, I was, like I said, just plain scared. Did this person live near me? Was there any potential way he could physically come to me? Was there a way I could reimagine the meaning of the gun? I never told my family about it. I was sad, so sad, to keep it from them, but they didn't deserve the installation of fear into their life. They didn't sign up for this show.

At what cost do we as a society normalize that anyone who goes on a TV show "deserves" this social media deluge? In a simplified show, there would be a T chart of villains and victims. Because I was seen as a villain, many comments on my social media platforms stated that I "knew" what I signed up for. That I wanted this fame, that I was a "clout chaser." To be honest, I still don't know what that is. What was I chasing? Well, a chance to work with an alleged top matchmaker who could find me my life partner. Certainly, my goal was not to be trolled relentlessly or to receive threats from men with guns. So, alone in bed that night, I reported the Facebook message to Facebook and then emailed a screen shot to Netflix. They had requested that we tell them if we were threatened. I was relieved to have them take this seriously.

I was still receiving an endless stream of press requests at the same time. There was no time for me to wallow in abusive threats. The trolls came after me every time an article came out, thinking I was paid for it. They also thought I was paid to participate in the show. Let me be clear: I was not paid. My intent when signing up for the show was to find love through a matchmaker's help. I paid thousands of dollars for my own hair, makeup, and outfits. I invested in being a participant by taking paid time off from my hectic job as general counsel of an insurance brokerage firm. I gave hundreds of hours of my time to international media outlets. I did this of my own choosing.

So here I sat with threats directed me, people taking pictures of my house as they lurked outside, and social networks that thrummed with a constant barrage of vitriol. The abuse—indeed, the threats—hurled my way were easy for people online to ignore or, worse, respond to with haughty comments that I asked for it when I signed up to be a on a show.

This leads me to question why, as a society, we tolerate this behavior. Why are women not heard and defended? For all our advances on issues of women's rights and bullying, online abuse of reality television participants is still regarded as par for the course.

But here's the thing: I am a lawyer in Houston, Texas. I point out the city and location because it's devoid of anything entertainment related. My world of peers had no idea about this industry, but we could certainly outline the years of training one needed to be a doctor or the amount of time lawyers spent on taking the bar exam. That was our world—medicine, law, oil and gas corporate jobs. I didn't know this could happen.

I began to dread going on social media. I'd hold my breath before reading any messages, so scared of what I might read. The messages were downright hateful, not only about my alleged "attitude" on the show but also about my mother, which hurt me in ways I can't begin to unpack even as I write this nine months later. It's one thing to throw me under a bus. It's quite another to throw my loving, kind, progressive, c'est la vie mother under one alongside me. I could handle it, or so I believed. I was to blame for being ignorant, or so I believed. I was stuck with my fate of being hated and reviled, or so I believed.

And to a certain extent, those facts are just that, facts. Years from now, someone will meet me for the first time at a dinner party and will dislike me because of my depiction on the show. Years from now, I will be sitting in a café and someone will whisper to their friend, "There's Aparna from that *Indian Matchmaking* show. She was such a cold bitch." And I have no control over those moments or those perceptions. Viewers binge-watched the show during a worldwide pandemic, took it as truth, and didn't think much about the show once they moved on to the next one. They'll only be reminded, even if it's years later, when they see me. That loss of control I have over my own story is truly the most defeating. The realization hits me in waves—sometimes suddenly and out of the blue. Sometimes in succession, leaving me feeling like I'm drowning.

But in those first weeks, as I held my breath before signing on to social media platforms, I tried to identify why I felt such dread. What was it that I was most afraid of reading? Because, quite quickly, I rationally understood that the hate spit my way was not because that person knows me—or in this case the real me. The person is reacting to the craftily edited likeness of me on the screen. I am secure in knowing who I am. And on the days when I faltered in that knowing after the show came out, my friends reminded me. They called me generous, loyal, warm, and loving. They acknowledged that yes, I also used sarcasm and had a penchant for saying the absurd, but that it was never unkind and always with a smile. That's until a camera crew comes in; tapes you for 150 hours; removes all those aspects of you that are generous, loyal, warm, and loving; and leaves in its place a version of you that is cut, chopped, and connected into 1.5 hours maximum. So let's review this: 150 hours of true self becomes 1.5 hours of the story arc they created.

In my further examination, there was certainly something that bothered me, and the reason behind my dread was both surprising and not: it's because I was waiting for someone to call me ugly. I was waiting for someone to take a screenshot of me on the show and announce that the reason I'm alone is because I am fat and ugly. Except, in the biggest turn of all, those comments never came—not in full force, anyway. People did comment on my teeth being crooked, but I easily dismissed it as petty. Even amid the online bullying and attacks on my character, I was flooded with relief.

But I couldn't just have relief and not examine why—because in my heart of hearts, I was disappointed that I cared about a keyboard warrior's comment on my physicality. Why is it that even a strong, secure woman's biggest fear is being called ugly and/or fat? Why do I—and so many women—harbor a deep-rooted need to be pretty and likeable to all men and to society as a whole? Of course, there is emotional baggage to unpack for every woman individually (myself included), but on a macro level, why can the worst insult hurled at a woman (especially in justifying why she's single) be the ever-simplified, "Oh, she's single because she's ugly." And they wouldn't mean ugly on the inside, which from my edit, I could arguably see their point. They would mean it on the outside, which is something I can't change. And believe me, I did my best to shield myself from those comments preemptively. I spent thousands on clothes, called on hair and makeup artists each day of taping, and obsessively styled clothes that would look best on camera—a.k.a. solids, bright colors, avoiding small prints or dots. The producers chuckled as I got ready for taping, assuring me that no one else was taking this to "this level." All my unnamed castmates around the world were appearing on camera as they would in their day-to-day life. I scoffed. At this point, even if one hundred people watched this docuseries, I was still not going to appear on camera without minimal help from hair and makeup professionals. Ax throwing or goat yoga, I was going to be ready regardless.

So here I was, bracing myself as I read comments and messages and moving through my own rooted pain of likeability and beauty from the span of my teens to my present-day unwitting public persona. Many a South Asian woman, and perhaps countless other women, can recall the definition of beauty in the early 2000s, when bony Abercrombie & Fitch models in ripped white tanks with their pelvic bones sticking out was the ideal. The boys in our classrooms pined for the girls who embodied that look, their stick-straight hair and fair skin only accentuating their lean figures. Let me tell you what I was: not lean, not White, and not beautiful to the young men I befriended but never dated. One or two would approach me here and there—an exotic deviation of their normal taste in girlfriends—but I knew the rarity of the situation when it presented itself. I knew I was the outsider. And in college, when I was first introduced to South Asians en masse, I quickly realized I didn't fit the standards of beauty outlined in South Asian culture (being "fair" and "thin"). Forget "White culture," I couldn't even live up to my own community's benchmarks. It was a losing battle that no amount of clothes styling or dieting could fix.

Now in my thirties, I am so glad for those losing battles. They taught me to move on from any attempts of mastering the ideal and to instead master myself just as I am. Said less opaquely, I started being more of myself—first out of a strange defeat and then later out of my desire to love myself as I am. I can't pin if it was age alone or time spent living in a world where I would not fit into the abstract likeabilty of the woman. In those years when I decided to forego even trying, I became strong, courageous, and, most important, open in sharing my thoughts, desires, and triumphs as well as my defeats. I sat on my couch in an orange dress and was able to easily respond to the question of how I feel when a man rejects me, coming from the producer sitting on a few crates behind the camera. How would I feel if a man didn't want me? I rolled my eyes internally, wanting to respond, "Just fine, thanks." But instead, I composed myself and said, "I actually don't mind being rejected. It is really not a thing that bothers me. It happens, right? People can like you and you can not like them, and vice versa. If someone doesn't like me, I think that's their problem, not mine, because I like me." It wasn't rehearsed. I hadn't thought about any hypothetical retort to such a question. I was just speaking from experience, from years of the world around me trying to make me feel like I wasn't enough. And here I was, still liking myself. Perhaps that's the moment we are in: we raised a generation of strong women who believe they can achieve anything and who also believe they deserve to be liked for who they are. The belief is worth everything.

5

BE LIKE APARNA

THERE'S ALWAYS SOME LIGHT in the darkness. In the early days of the Twitter hate storm, one tweet stood out to me. A woman, a total stranger in a small town in India, listed my dislikes: "Aparna doesn't like beaches. Aparna doesn't want kids around since they're noisy. Aparna is 'stubborn' and has 'high standards.' Aparna is 'negative.' Aparna is hard to please." The woman capped it off with "I'm Aparna. You should be too." The tweet's message is clear: it encourages women to feel free to be opinionated and decisive, to dare to like—and dislike—whatever they want. At the time, it was also pushback on the matchmaker's characterization of me as "stubborn" and "negative." I began messaging this woman, and she shared that she is a teacher to young women. She loved my portrayal on the show and saw it as a necessary representation on the screens of South Asian women in India. She told me there is no one like me on their televisions in their living rooms. And that seeing me empowered them to speak their own minds not only about matchmaking but also about their status in the workplace, in schools, and in their family's homes.

The support did not end there. South Asian women in Pakistan and India begin championing my strength and decisiveness. Within days, women started to take back the word *stubborn*.

Stubborn became a compliment for women who refuse to back down, who ask for what they want, and who truly feel they deserve it—in the matchmaking process and in life. These women reached out to me on Instagram with harrowing tales of their own Sima aunties—women who demeaned them for their looks or their education or their age when tasked with matchmaking them. Women who portrayed themselves as well-meaning aunties but instead took every opportunity to tear down women into submissive brides-to-be. Women who had no intention to listen to their wants and needs for a life partner. Women in South Asia were all too familiar with this figure in their lives, and they were done with it. It was surprising to me initially, because I was so acutely unaware of the persistent traumas inflicted on women in South Asia surrounding arranged marriages. So many of them asked me why I would even subject myself to such a demeaning and oppressive process. But for me, matchmaking was just another opportunity to meet somebody. I was open to meeting people at a wedding, in the grocery store, or on a dating application. So when the chance came to work with an alleged "world-renowned matchmaker," for me it was just another tool to utilize in the construction of finding my life partner. I had never before thought of what it meant to millions of women across the world from me.

Here's what I did know. These South Asian women were thrilled to see themselves represented on their TVs. They couldn't believe there was a Netflix show with a cast of Indian people that aired in almost every country in the world (those that allow Netflix). But they also hated the show and shared their thoughts profusely in public places. So many were triggered, they said. So many could not make it through the first episode, they said. So many despised the show for the way it represented their culture to the outside world. They wanted more. They wanted less. It was exhausting, especially to me, since I clearly had no ability to control the editing of the show. We were too rich. We were too educated. We were all Hindu. We were not dark enough. We were heterosexual. But here's where I will defend *Indian Matchmaking*: It never claimed to be the one show that would represent a billion-plus people in India and millions more outside its borders. It was simply a show about one matchmaker and her seven alleged clients in India and the United States. The show was composed of only those experiences—not the totality of all South Asian arranged marriage experiences.

So I think it did what it set out to do. It started conversations about our culture that were difficult for many people, and the parts of it they didn't appreciate were highlighted in these short eight episodes. Many years from now, I believe we will look back at 2020 as just the beginning of South Asian media being represented on widespread global streaming platforms. In comparison, at one point in time, many of us outside the Black community in the United States watched *The Cosby Show* and *The Fresh Prince of Bel-Air*, naively assuming that they, along with rap videos, made up Black culture. We were very wrong, clearly. And as more Black media proliferated on mainstream channels, we outside the community saw Black America as nuanced, complex, full of its own diverse culture. One day, after *Never Have I Ever* and *Indian Matchmaking* have long passed, we will have many more representations of this culture for others to consume. We will have shows and movies and cartoons that add constantly to the layered content that is available for everyone to build their understanding of what it means to be South Asian—be it in India or its diaspora.

I saw the conversations starting in my own DMs after the show launched. Messages poured in from Europe and the United States, mostly from people of Caucasian descent. They had surprises of their own when they watched *Indian Matchmaking*. They shared with me that they had always assumed "arranged marriage" meant "forced marriage." It was shocking for them to see that we were all given a choice to say yes or no to our prospective suitors. And so began my explanation of arranged marriage to them—mostly highlighting that each person's understanding of it was totally different than anyone else's. We have "fingerprint" definitions, meaning they are unique to each one of us. Even though I grew up mainly in the United States, my understanding of arranged marriage is totally different than Manisha's or Nadia's or even Vyasar's concept of this tradition.

Four factors influence people's views on arranged marriage: First is physical geography. Where did the person grow up? What shaped their ideas of dating norms? What weddings did they watch on television? What books did they read that highlighted cultural norms? I grew up mainly in Houston, Texas. I read the Baby-Sitters Club and Sweet Valley High novels. I watched *Saved by the Bell* and revered movies like *The Sound of Music*, where Maria ultimately gets married in a white dress with a long veil. In my world, my access to media informed my understanding of love and marriage. Imagine how different that list would look for Ankita or Pradhyuman from where they sit in Delhi and Mumbai, respectively.

Second, we must take into account our peers. When we started learning about dating, what was the norm in our peer groups? At what age did we start receiving those first kisses, seeing couples pair up, and later, begin to see long-term relationships form? What stories did we hear about how people's parents met and got married? What did we believe was the "right time" to consider these factors to begin with? I went to public schools in Houston, Texas. My classmates were diverse—White, Asian, Latino/Latina, and Black. We saw our first boyfriend–girlfriend pairings in fourth grade, saw them appear more rampantly by seventh grade, and believed we would find our happily ever after with the perfect guy (or girl). There was no talk of arranged marriage in the schoolyard or by the lockers. There was no question we would choose our own life partners one day. Again, is that true for every one of my castmates? Most decidedly not. They had their own informed ideas about marriage based on their individual friend groups and school environments.

Third, we reflect on our families and their attitudes about arranged marriage. We also look to their experiences of it and their understanding of the whole process. My mother had an unsuccessful arranged marriage to a man who had nothing in common with her. It was a poor match, and that's being charitable in its description. Had someone told her that her own daughter would attempt to use a matchmaker, she would have scoffed and said it wasn't possible. Yet here we were on a matchmaking show based in the United States (for my participation anyway). However, it was on my terms and under the guise of progressive ideals where each participant had a say in their own match. So she supported me, dubiously at first but then with a full grasp that I would not be pushed into any situation I did not want to be in—a far cry from her own run-in with a traditional arranged marriage at the age of nineteen. And sure enough, when Sima showed her true colors in berating me for being "too powerful" in my own matchmaking process, my mother was the first to tell me I was free to exit the situation. She told Sima, and she told me—her very intention was to make me powerful. That was certainly not going to change. When Sima pushed back and chided my mother for not forcibly exerting her power of "persuasion" over my matches, my mother was absolutely horrified. She made it clear that Sima's mentality was not conducive to our family's sensibilities. Preach on, Mom. Preach on.

The show included interviews of happily married couples who met through an arranged marriage process. As I see it, the show was littered with these examples of dripping sweetness and shared giggles between the couples to influence the viewers' perception of arranged marriage. From where I stand, it's hard to forget all the layers of sexism, feminism, casteism, and colorism (not to mention heightism) that line the roads to these matches.

Let's move on to the fourth and final factor in the creation of the "fingerprint" definition of arranged marriage: you. More specifically, it's your opinion of how much of a say you should have in choosing your life partner. I had a strong idea of what I wanted in my future life partner and an equally strong desire to share it with my matchmaker, whom I mistakenly believed was on my team. When I found not a teammate but only a critic, I still shared my wants freely because I believed that was part of the process. I believed my voice was the ultimate choice maker. I still believe that today. No matter how I meet my future partner, I will be the final arbiter of whether he is right for me. And he will be the final arbiter of whether I am right for him. That is my understanding of the world, and it makes up the fourth factor of my definition of arranged marriage.

For the viewer, I was given a direct counterpart in contradiction, otherwise known as the portrayal of Akshay in Mumbai. In the show, you see a young man with glazed-over eyes who comments offhand that he wants a woman who embodies his mom's best qualities. Let's pause here. English is not his native language, as fluent as he might be in it. And even if he's spoken English from a young age, he does not speak American English. He shared later on a reunion interview that he *meant* to articulate that there were many qualities in his mother that he admired and would like to see in his future partner. Regardless of intent, in my opinion, the viewers saw Akshay as a young man with no backbone or ability to stand up to his family's pressures, specifically his mother's. And then I was shown to be the "picky" and "stubborn" older woman who had too many ideas of what she wanted in a partner. We all know now that Sima disapproved of my vocal point of view and spoke freely of her disapproval on and off camera, to my family's face and behind their backs, while taping her master interviews. But I still have my own definition of arranged marriage, and I continue today to forge ahead with that very understanding.

With that "Be Like Aparna" tweet trending in certain online forums, I made a "Be Like Aparna" T-shirt that many women across the world ordered. They wanted to make the statement and, even more concisely, wear the statement. It was a battle cry, and I was so touched. I was also astounded by the support I received in the press. It's almost like they lived in a different world than the one bombarding me on social media platforms. Well, not almost—they *did* live in a different world. Many of you saw some of the articles, some of the videos, some of the podcasts. Some of you saw a lot of them. And here's what I experienced from doing extensive interviews: It was the women who stuck up for me. It was the female journalists I met through the promotion period (and beyond) who amplified my voice time and again. It was these women who took my edited self and highlighted its unfair angling and tired villainous tropes. They individually did more than I could ever do myself on my own social media platforms. They gave me a voice. From high school newspapers to the *New York Times*, the women journalists who emailed me, DM'ed me, or contacted me through official Netflix channels were my champions. They lent me an opportunity to tell my own story, and they painted it artfully within the context of Indian culture and its tradition of arranged marriage. I stand here today forever grateful to these women and forever certain that the clichéd "women helping women" mantra is indeed the way we will all rise. It's the epitome of the saying "A rising tide lifts all boats." And I was lifted high. I was relieved to know there were people in this crazy world of voracious media consumption who were thoughtful and insightful.

On the heels of a powerful article in my defense, *Vulture* published a second article dedicated to what I don't like, from my university's cafeteria food to the countries I mentioned on my dates to Dilip and Shekar. It was not lost on me that this tongue-in-cheek list further reinforced the show's pigeonholing of me as picky and negative. Let's not forget, that easily could have been angled as discerning and direct—but wasn't. The article was written by a man; notably, it was one of the only articles about me that was written by a man. In my mind, some poor junior writer (or even an intern) was given the assignment of going through *Indian Matchmaking* episodes one through five, the "Aparna" episodes, and documenting each of my dislikes. He did his job well. Either his name was the one on the byline or he lurked in the background while given this menial assignment.

Regardless, it prompted me to pose the question: Why didn't the show (and *Vulture*) list all the things I *love*? As a multifaceted woman, I have a long list of likes and dislikes—I do, after all, know my mind. And in the hundred plus hours of film footage, I am certain I decisively stated things I love. I do that in my everyday life—many of us do. We state what we do and do not like. Some would argue it's healthy and a part of boundary setting. I don't like ice in my water. I do like hugs. I don't like the window seat on a plane. I do like family dinners with no phones. The reason my likes weren't included seems obvious to me: presenting me as someone who also enjoys a lot of things wouldn't match the vilified archetype of the successful-and-difficult career woman—not for the showrunners, the press, or society. Yes, *Vulture* wrote a feature article supporting me. But it also leapt at the opportunity to use the show's archetype to publish another article mocking my outlined dislikes. This article was shared by one of my high school classmates who also tagged me on Facebook, so it appears on my own timeline. Friends who went to high school with us, as well as people I do not know personally, instantly liked it. It's such a small thing. But it felt personal and I felt embarrassed, cringing at the article being featured on my own wall. Hating that it had a place on "my property." Knowing I couldn't delete it now that it had been liked by so many people. I took a deep breath and typed out a blasé comment, acknowledging the article's humor.

Did the person who shared the article and all the people who liked it realize its implications? Did they see how the article failed to capture me as a whole person, how it furthered harmful stereotypes and discouraged women from speaking up? It seems they did not. It dawned on me right then that in today's world, a decisive woman who can identify her "likes and dislikes" might still be judged for her opinions. The only alternative is not having an opinion at all. And for me, that just won't do.

6

REFUSE TO LET YOURSELF
BE ERASED FROM
YOUR OWN STORY

SOMEONE ASKED ME what my turning point was—the moment I knew I had to take matters into my own hands. Candidly, it was the death threat. It shook me in ways I can never fully explain. I'm relieved that 99.9999 percent of people in the world will never know the sickening feeling of that very moment. But here's what I realized then. While I would never have the reach of an international show to create my own public persona, I did have my voice and an ability to share my version of reality with the media and on my own social media platforms. Everyone had some advice to give. I spoke to a "crisis management" publicist referred to me through a friend of a friend. He was an older White man, deeply entrenched in the industry and hardly phased by my depiction on the show. In fact, after a quick Twitter trending hashtag review and an Instagram skim-over, he declared that he saw no crisis. The press had already shown up on my "side," and here, at week two, I only had to ride it out. He advised I craft a delicate balance of not being defensive but also explaining my perspective to the media and on my social media platforms. I should gently remind everyone that reality television is expertly edited with very little accuracy in general.

I knew he was right, but I felt so overwhelmed by this new industry that neither I nor my Houston close friends were familiar with. I started reaching out to friends in California, and they had more contacts for me. I spoke to publicists but eventually decided I didn't need a traditional one. First, they charged $15,000 or more for a three-month retainer, and second, I had more than enough press coverage opportunities coming to me organically. I didn't need them to use their networks to get me additional outlets. I then connected with other female reality stars with strong personalities or vilified portrayals, including Jessica Batten of *Love Is Blind* and Olivia Caridi from *The Bachelor*. These women are kind and compassionate and truly understand my unique position. They also confirmed something I had never fully considered before: the vilification I was experiencing from the world had happened before on reality television—countless times. The way I saw it, I was ready to use all my resources and skills to tell our *collective* story. I also knew I had to speak up for the women to come. The strong, determined, practical, and ambitious women who would be the next "villains" on the next show. The ones the world would watch and think, "Oh, she deserves every poor outcome that comes her way in life (and love), because she is unlikeable."

Let me make this very clear. In my opinion, it is no coincidence that Jessica Batten was vilified on television with untrue narratives and crafty editing of her personality. She was, if you're taking note, the only woman on the show who had her own home, a sweet dog, and a six-figure income. She was beautiful and looking for her own partner in life, but according to the stereotypes that "sell" or have increased viewership, this honest portrayal of her just wouldn't cut it. We instead had to be presented with a story line far from the truth and editing that strung together her least favorable moments completely out of context. I saw memes when *Indian Matchmaking* came out that showed "Jessica, 34" next to "Aparna, 34"—begging the viewer to vote on who was worse. Who deserved love less? And who was more unlikeable? "Neither" is the correct answer, but the keyboard warriors did not get it right. Both are women who love their families, excel in their careers, have healthy and loving friendships, have a pet they love—and yes, want to find love.

Believe it or not, you as a viewer are constantly consuming stories on your television that oversimplify people into tropes and stereotypes.

Let's see if *Indian Matchmaking* is an example of such over-simplification. I'll give you my personal take on it—the Aparna breakdown, if you will. First, draw a T chart: label the first column VILLAINS and the second column VICTIMS. I believe every person on this show fits into one of these columns. I am in the VILLAINS column. Every man I dated was thus a victim (of my villainous ways). Nadia was a victim. Every man she dated (except for the unfinished ending with Shekar) was thus a villain. Let's summarize my take here.

Villains	Victims
Me	Nadia
My mother	Vyasar
Pradhyuman	Srini (the irony of all ironies)
Akshay	Shekar
Akshay's mother	Dilip (a.k.a., every man who
Guru	went on a date with me)
Vinay	Rupam
Manisha	
Richa	

Let's go a step further. Rupam, one of my absolute favorites, is an incredible woman. She is strong, fiercely loyal to her family, and happily in love with her own match from Bumble. In real life, she is a highly accomplished pediatric allergy doctor with advanced training in dermatology. She is a no-nonsense, pragmatic, and independent woman. She is by no means the victim the media made her out to be when the show aired. She is a woman who is thriving in a life that is fully aligned with her values and solidly reflective of her own self-worth.

So what is the show really about? It's about seven singles with one unsuccessful matchmaker who all went on lackluster dates with people who weren't right for them. Shekar and I went on a few dates. We were certain there was no chemistry, but we knew we got along well. To this day, we remain really good friends. We speak on the phone for hours at least a few times a week and text back and forth all the time. I go to him for dating advice, and he comes to me for the same. The same goes for Dilip and me, and Jay and me. We are all friends. In fact, those three guys started a group text called Aparna's Guys and are independently communicating without me being involved. And I love it. For me, that's what the show was ultimately about. I met (mostly) nice South Asian men also looking for love and not finding it with me or anyone else on the show. But we respected each other enough to stay connected and even start long-lasting friendships with each other.

I had a moment of personal reckoning when I heard Vinay's story on his social media platform. I went to my two best friends, who taped the living room "Fat Pants Friday" with me and the dinner scene where they met Jay, and asked them point-blank, "If I asked you to re-create a scene where Jay ghosted me, would you sit at a restaurant and pretend he was coming?" They answered quickly, "No. Never. And honestly, Aparna, we would pull you aside and tell you it's unacceptable to do the same, even without us." They explained that they would have strongly advised me not to be a part of any such taping, should it have been presented to me. I also asked Shekar whether he and his two friends would have re-created such a scene. "Without a doubt, no," he replied. "And if I did it without my friends, they would likely no longer call themselves my friends." I had my answer. I needed to hear it from external sources. My own moral compass needed to be steadied on true north.

To this day, Vinay receives unjustifiable negative messages and is bad-mouthed on social media platforms. I believe one thing wholeheartedly—there are no bad people, only bad decisions. We all make our choices. I continue to receive hateful messages about my alleged treatment of Srini. I still wish I could respond to every one of them that I was hurt by Srini and his demeaning behavior. But I know it's also futile. It's my personal belief that the journey of looking for love is a tough one for everyone. It always comes with its share of heartache and soul-crushing moments. Even I, who was portrayed as strong and decisive, had a terrible date—one that left in me in tears and ready to walk away from the show altogether.

Ask yourself this: Who curates and benefits from the story lines that are created on unscripted shows? Go a step further and ask, for all so-called reality television you consume: What information is missing? Who stands the most to gain from you not receiving that information? I understand this is entertainment, and I fully support it for that one function. But am I upset that people believe *Indian Matchmaking* to be true? Yes. Do I blame these viewers? On a bad day, yes. I do blame them for their ignorance in the way they consume media. Is that fair? Probably not, but I'm being honest here.

The first week I moved to New York City, I met a nice guy at a dinner with mutual friends. He is educated, handsome, single . . .

and very much slipped in some of his impressions of my castmates. That one was "sweet." The other "a teddy bear." What he didn't say was what he thought of me. He had enough manners to omit that impression. So here was a peer of mine, in a new social situation for me, and even he had ideas surrounding who we were as people based on our depiction on television. I was blunt when I told him in a moment of weakness, "I'm honestly shocked that someone as intelligent as you would not realize there is little to no truth to what you watched on television and yet you processed it as some sort of truth." He looked surprised but then shrugged and said, "Well honestly, I just didn't think too hard about it. I watched it in two nights and didn't process much after I turned it off."

And that's the crux of it. No one processes much. That's the business model. The entertainment industry is doubling down on it. And we as a global community and as consumers of their product should say we will not stand for this anymore. We, as a society, are better than this. In light of the Black Lives Matter and Me Too movements, in an era where we push for equality and authenticity, let's ask ourselves why we still consume entertainment as truth. I am not saying we do away with "unscripted" television. I am saying we speak more about its context and its purpose. I understand too that this is an uphill battle. That my one voice is just a whisper in a din of fast, frenzied streams of more and more shows being produced and aired each week with more rounds of villains and victims. Of heroes and antiheroes. Of princesses and ogres.

———————

At the head of it all in *Indian Matchmaking*, there was Sima, who brought her own beliefs to the table. Steeped in her own cultural norms and her general disdain for a woman who was strong enough to express what she wanted from her future partner, to many viewers, she reinforced the ugliness of South Asian patriarchal culture. South Asians around the world were triggered by her direct words and her underlying sentiments that it was a woman's exclusive obligation to "adjust and compromise." But let's be clear, her misogyny is not isolated. News outlets and social media platforms called it misogyny. I had to ask myself later, many months after the show aired, *Were these comments and behaviors just sexist? Or were they straight-up misogyny?* Until it was blatantly hurled at me on camera, I had never stopped to consider the distinction. I researched; I read. I strived to understand *what* had happened to me.

One article summed it up best. I won't pretend to expound expert views on this vast topic but will instead share with you what resonated most with me. In a simple Q&A format interview in *Vox*, Sean Illing asks Kate Manne, a Cornell philosophy professor, about the difference between sexism and misogyny. She breaks it down into their easily digestible connection and functions. Manne says, "Misogyny is *not* about male hostility or hatred toward women—instead, it's about controlling and punishing women who challenge male dominance. Misogyny rewards women who reinforce the status quo and punishes those who don't."

She goes on to clarify, "I think most misogynistic behavior is about hostility toward women who violate patriarchal norms and expectations, who aren't serving male interests in the ways they're expected to. So there's this sense that women are doing something wrong: that they're morally objectionable or have a bad attitude or they're abrasive or shrill or too pushy. But women only appear that way because we expect them to be otherwise, to be passive."

Sexism, according to Manne, is the "patriarchal social structures, [and] bastions of male privilege where a dominant man might feel entitled to (and often receive) feminine care and attention from women." So in essence, "Sexism is the ideology that *supports* patriarchal social relations, but misogyny *enforces* it when there's a threat of that system going away."

I got it. It was my *aha* moment. My being unlikeable to Sima *and* to many viewers was because of their conscious and unconscious misogyny. By way of example, after my first two dates with Srini and Raj—both forty-one years old and both years away (if ever) from wanting a committed relationship leading to marriage—I was asked by a producer what I wanted in my next matches. I told her I wanted matches who were closer to my age. I was thirty-four at the time and was hoping to find someone who didn't have a perennial desire to remain a bachelor. She scoffed. "Forty-one is your demographic. Men who are younger than that want women much younger than you." I looked at her in disbelief. Here was a lovely, strong female producer who, in my mind, was on "my team." She wanted for me what I wanted for me—whatever that may be. I questioned her, "Why couldn't I date someone a few years older than me, or even a couple of years younger than me?" She doubled down. "Because they don't want a thirty-four-year-old. You want to get married and likely have kids soon. They don't want to take that on. They're men. They don't want that pressure."

I searched her face for a smile or an indication she was kidding. She was dead serious. Because in her world, I was being unrealistic as a thirty-four year old *woman* with a biological clock for wanting to be with someone close to my own age. I knew even then—and in hindsight it's even clearer—that this woman meant well. Her intentions were in the right place. Her goal was the same as mine—to find me a partner who would be on the same page as me, someone who wanted a committed relationship. But wow, did it sting to hear those comments. For a moment, I was honestly shaken and fearful that there was truth to her statements, but then

I reminded myself that I deserved whatever I asked for—and that in fact, a man my age was not asking for "too much" for myself. It was merely my preference, and I had a right to express it.

But that's what Manne was talking about in her *Vox* article: society's cultural norms of a woman being sweet, kind, and paternalistic *are* sexist. The enforcement of those beliefs, in this case that I would be "flexible" and "adjust," or be resigned to being matched with men in their forties, was the misogyny coming into play—the enforcement of sexist beliefs that this limited voice was all I deserved in matchmaking. At the time, I didn't even see it. I was pining too hard for a successful outcome and too hard to draw adequate boundaries for any defeating and overwhelming behavior toward me. Now I ask myself about these broad topics and the way they flit in and out of every woman's world, probably daily. How many other women are coerced by those in power to accept ideas about a woman's place in society that they do not inherently believe themselves? Ideas that diminish their existence and, yes, erase their voice? More than I can count, I'm certain, and the idea of it makes me feel overwhelmed and defeated. But as we taped the show, I honestly didn't consider any of these macro topics that are ingrained in our routines and spaces. I was lost in the first-time overstimulation of having fourteen people in my life (and home) taping me for ten hours a day.

It took the launch of the show and the endless streams of press in that summer of 2020 for me to assert my own voice. One day, my daily Google Alert for the show identified an article in which Smriti is discussing how much she loves Aparna. When asked by the media outlet if "the show was not edited to fit a narrative as Aparna suggests [in other press]," Smriti responds, "For the most part, Aparna does stand behind everything that was said and done on the show." I was livid. I screenshotted that portion of the article and sent it to Smriti, telling her not to speak on my behalf to the press. Smriti apologized for being out of bounds, and while I accepted the apology, I was not effusive in my tone. I reminded Smriti to speak only for herself in the future. I'd experienced more than enough of my voice being erased in this narrative and would not have it anymore. I was setting strong boundaries about how my own story would be heard, and I made it clear to myself—and others—that I would directly go after anyone who hindered my own storytelling. The painful lesson learned with empowerment as the final result? In a world where the voices of the privileged and dominant stamp out the voices of minorities, make yourself heard. Make them listen. And tell your own damn narrative.

7

A DAILY AFFIRMATION:
BUT *I* LIKE ME

THERE ARE SOME ASPECTS of *Indian Matchmaking* that I am more than relieved to *not* be a part of. And there is one contributor none of us have met who is at the center of it all: Richa. Anonymous, never to be heard from again, never known to begin with: Richa. In the last five minutes of the last episode, the viewers meet a thirty-year-old in San Diego, California, who blew up the internet with her comments on what she wants in a future husband. Or more accurately, she blew up the internet with the one comment she made about wanting a husband who was "not too dark, you know? Like fair-skinned." Crickets chirped before the tweeting screams began. And then, it never slowed down. I contextualized this woman to media outlets when it was brought up—this woman I had never met, whose last name I still don't know, and whom I may never meet. The truth is, if you're a part of the South Asian diaspora, you are too aware of the flippancy associated with these statements, mostly because they were always directed at you.

First, let's start with why I "defend" her. *Defend* is a loose term for explaining what I believe to be the heart (and historical significance) of those comments. In my understanding of South Asian immigrant beginnings in the United States, many of the people who came to this country were highly educated and were either students or professionals from India who came looking for opportunities. They were often from middle-class to lower-class backgrounds (not always, but from what I've read, that was the norm) and they retained their beliefs in a new country far from home. Remember, this was an era when phone calls "home" were not possible, when snail mail in the form of aerograms was infrequent, and when American news outlets didn't cover anything happening in India. These new immigrants were isolated and largely clung to their culture, as if it were frozen in time on the day they left. Indians in India may have progressed and moved on from the beliefs of the 1970s and 1980s, but these newfound Americans did not. The prevalent idea of colorism, that the lighter your skin, the more beautiful you are considered, lingered. I am by no means suggesting it does not exist in India today, mind you. I merely understand the theory that South Asian immigrants gripped tightly to their values-based ideas when they moved to the United States, and that included their beliefs surrounding beauty. So when Richa spoke to Sima candidly, she included this preference that she most likely heard in her own home from her own parents her whole life. Yes, she was born in the United States. Yes, she likely went to diverse schools. Yes, she should be more sensitive and aware about the implications of her statements. But the fact remains that when discussing marriage and partnerships, many of us grew up hearing such comments about color. And maybe, in some cases, those comments created what were considered preferences, like those Richa described to Sima on screen.

I told you *defend* was a loose term, didn't I? I just "lawyered" a supposition here with vague terms and lots of caveats, but it's one I had to point out as the judgment swirled darkly around the topic post–show launch. No pun intended, of course. But above all else, I recognize one thing: this is a heavy topic and one I am no expert on. All I know is that I was called "dark" and "short" my whole life. So anecdotally, I can speak to the prevalence of these hurtful statements. And yes, they're hurtful to the five-year-old who hears it, the twenty-year-old who hears it, and even the thirty-five-year-old who hears it. I don't recall when I first heard someone call me "dark," but I was aware of this fact as early as age four. We lived in Dubai when I was a child, in a very insular business community of Indians and Pakistanis. Higher education in our parents' generation was close to nil, and the backward mentalities of an India that favored lighter skin and height, especially in women, prevailed. I was born in London, and the favorite cluck of a tongue centered on questions about me being darker complexioned than my sister, who incidentally was born in Dubai. I asked my mother about this when I was older and heard the retelling of these comments, "Why didn't you just respond that skin color has nothing to do with the city you happened to be born in?" She told me it just wasn't worth her time to explain away uneducated comments. She's a better woman than me. I would have set the record straight. But I was only six when I left Dubai—not yet a "record straightener."

And so it went in that society. I was not as pretty as my sister, because she had cocoa-colored eyes, cheeks that were pink after playing on the jungle gym, and translucence to her skin that can't be gained through any beauty product on the market. After a long day at the country club pool, I would be an even deep brown color, while she would turn a golden shade reminiscent of the sun-kissed Barbies we played with before bed. I was slathered in sunscreen, told to spend less time in the sun, and encouraged to play fewer outdoor sports. I heard the nannies being told we should go to the private-compound parks at sunset for the last of the day's light. I heard the aunties cluck over my dark brown hair and compare it to my sister's light brown locks. Children do indeed absorb the chatter. Psychological studies and the endless stream of parenting books nowadays show that to be true. But in the 1980s in Dubai, no one knew. And no one cared. Life was a spectator sport full of commentary for things ranging from someone else's daughter's skin color to whether they would one day be as tall as their mother.

It didn't help that my mother was considered the epitome of "fair and lovely." At a stately five foot seven and always in heels, she towered over men and women alike in the South Asian community in Dubai. Impeccably dressed and never in the sun, she was a model example of what to be. Really, a true model. She even went to a finishing school in London in her late teens that taught her to model and walk with grace, and topped off her education with basic art history and formal dinner etiquette. It was an education on how to be a well-rounded wife-to-be for a lucky man. I didn't know any of this context when I was a child—only that she was the most beautiful woman in the world whose eyes crinkled when she smiled and whose perfectly formed lips were always the most delicious pink. She gave the best hugs and had the sweetest smile on her face every time she was with my sister and me. It's the knowledge you glean over time that settles into a full narrative of beauty and color and what it means to have both—or neither.

For most of my life, I would have neither. Repeatedly reminded by family acquaintances and friends alike that I was the darker one, the shorter one, and the less attractive should have broken me. But I processed what I thought was a fact and moved on with the things I loved. Those things included an interest in clothes that was strong by second grade. It might have even started much earlier. My family tells a story of me at age three receiving a designer outfit from a visitor who brought it from a chic children's boutique in England where she lived. I rejected the outfit outright, straight to this kind woman's face, immediately spitting out, "I will not wear this trouser dress." I could not be cajoled to even thank her. I was in a "dresses only" phase at the tender age of three, and I would not be swayed. When we moved to New York when I was in second grade, my mother introduced us to Gap Kids and Limited Too. Things weren't the same for years. I had to have my pink velvet stirrup leggings, my black sweater with knit neon bows, and the matching headband. I had to have the exact wardrobe I deemed appropriate. I was indulged and I enjoyed my closet, visiting it every day to lovingly pick out the next day's outfit. I still end my day by hanging up my clothes and examining my closets. When I picked out a house for myself, I even converted one room, the aforementioned closet room, into a salon of sorts where I could display my shoes, jewelry, and seasonal collections for me to assess easily. My love for my clothes started young, like I said. I can't help but think part of it was a rebellion for not being pretty enough or fair enough. At least I could control being well dressed. In a world where you're judged for physical traits you can't change, there were a few things you could do for yourself.

I was always buying small things to make me feel more put-together. When Cher in *Clueless* applied her lipstick with a brush from a small pot, I nagged my family for weeks to add it to the presents under the tree. I was twelve. I had never worn makeup in my life, but I knew I had to have the brush application to swipe a soft pink over my lips before first period and after lunch. I was adamant. And they caved. Clinique lip gloss pots with brushes were gifted to me, as requested. I used them every day for the next semester.

And it wasn't just about controlling the external. It became a whole package of making myself "better." Again, I am still uncertain whether this was all about negative comments about my skin color or height, but those two factors certainly played a part in my love for heels and obsession with not repeating outfits within four weeks. It also allowed me so much freedom. That's right. I was granted the space to read voraciously and not be bothered by activities I didn't enjoy, like ballet or playing with dolls with other girls. I got a public library card when we first moved to the States and visited every week. I would take the largest reusable tote with me, it sweeping down to the side of my knees, knocking into them when it was filled with the books from that week's dive into a new series. I gobbled American youth literature—learning about this country through the Baby-Sitters Club, the Boxcar Children, Nancy Drew, the Hardy Boys, and classics like *Little House on the Prairie* and *Anne of Green Gables* (yes, I know Anne lived in Canada).

I learned how to converse with adults and dine at restaurants alongside my mother. When we moved to New York City, my mom's friends were her younger brother's crew. She was about thirty-two and he was twenty-six, with their friends in between that age range. So while she was married at nineteen and had two children by the age of twenty-five, these thriving urban dwellers were living their single lives—or at least their childless adventuring days—in the city that never sleeps. They would take us along with them, my sister and I sitting down for fancy multicourse meals or for delicious Chinese food from a hole-in-the-wall with a group of gregarious, charming "aunties and uncles." We were their kids. These hardworking investment bankers and journalists and marketing geniuses spoiled us silly. They took us ice-skating around the Rockefeller Center tree in the winter, to Central Park for pretzels and Cokes in the summer, and showed us an endlessly entertaining city every day in between. On Halloween, when they had their house party to gather in costumes of black cats and masked heroes, they paused to walk us down their apartment floor for trick-or-treating. And when we hit unprepared yuppies, one after another, they took my sister and me up and down the elevator until we had our pumpkins filled with candy bars, random kitchen snacks, and cash from their neighbors. These family friends were our posse. We didn't have iPads, we weren't left at home (most of the time), and we were included.

My sister and I grew up well socialized, to say the least. And this ease with diverse groups transferred to school. Both popular in our own right, we made friends easily and enjoyed our groups in the classroom. Teachers told our mother at parent-teacher conferences that if they had classrooms full of Aparnas/Vansas, they would be thrilled. We were insulated in a bubble of love and nurturing for our entire childhood in the United States. Away from the glaring eyes of a narrow-minded community, we were free to be. Just be.

I only became friends with other South Asians in the last few years of high school. Most of my early teens were spent with friends from all backgrounds. I lived in a predominantly Jewish neighborhood and went to twenty-six bar and bat mitzvahs at age thirteen. I begged for one for myself, but my mom firmly retorted I would have to wait for my sweet sixteen birthday since, well, we weren't Jewish. Understandable. My point is that I had been mostly shielded, unintentionally, from the mutters of my Dubai childhood about my skin color.

But when I joined a Hindi language class in high school and met other Indian kids born and brought up here in the States, I was surprised to hear *kalu* as a slur slipping so easily out of their mouths. The native speakers who were in the class for an easy A+ mocked the Catholic, Malayalam students in Hindi, mostly targeting their darker skin tones. I was shocked. I kept my distance but understood quite quickly that the judgment was present. And that I was not fair enough to be considered pretty. It was the most bony girls, and the ones who were a few shades lighter than me, who would be labeled as the "prize girlfriends." Those girls giggled endlessly, tamed their unruly eyebrows with constant threading, and only dated other South Asian boys. I was too busy to bother with their exclusion of me. I ran for school government positions, took only college-level courses, volunteered at a domestic violence nonprofit, was editor of the school newspaper, and got a retail job at a nearby clothing boutique. But I heard them. I heard them loud and clear.

College was the solidification of what I knew all along. I was not fair enough, tall enough, or lean enough to be beautiful according to the South Asians. I was by no means ever called an ugly duckling. But when I bemoaned that "the cute Indian guy in my economics class wasn't into me," I was told by my Indian friends to expect more of that, since I wasn't the standard of beauty. I would never be that standard either. I understood that implicitly, and while I kept my eye out for a South Asian guy who piqued my interest, I somehow always found myself with men of different races. Ones who appreciated my beauty as it stood, ones who respected my many groups of different friends, ones who loved how different I was from those "other Indian girls." I found men who were interested in curing cancer, patenting their robotic thesis projects, and . . . me. That was enough for me. Sure, I knew I was looking for a South Asian guy eventually, but since I wasn't "tall, slim, and trim" in the words of Sima Taparia (and everyone else in the community), it seemed I would have to wait on that guy. So I lived my life, again with that freedom. And now, I wasn't just reading all the time—I was exploring the world for months at time. When I traveled the world in a ship for one hundred days, I avoided the hottest part of the day and its equator-strong sun while cruising. But that also meant I avoided my friends who sat on the top deck all afternoon, sunbathing with textbooks lying on their swimsuit-clad chests as they dozed. I would sit alone under the shaded deck with a smoothie and study in the dining chairs around the café tables, watching them from afar and meandering their direction when they took study breaks to chat. I avoided excursions that had me in my swimsuit for too long—that was just an opportunity for me to turn shades darker than the day before, and I wasn't having it. The one other South Asian girl in the program (also named Aparna, which caused endless confusion for our peers) also avoided the sun but without much envy for the others, without the disappointment or feelings of being left out that I was racked with each day. Indiscriminate with her friends and happy to mill about the interior common areas of the ship, the other Aparna would flit up to the sunny decks for a few minutes before returning inside without a backward glance. My own group of close friends were always lying out on the deck chairs, though, so I felt my separation from them intensely.

My small rebellion started slowly, more than 75 percent into our journey. I began with lunches on the deck, the wind whipping our hair into our food as the boat moved quickly onward to the next country. The salt from the ocean next to us would leave a light layer on the utensils going into our mouth and on the cups we sipped from. We had never been happier, all of us dining under the blue sky that reflected the same blue of the ocean. I had never been more carefree. By the time we reached our last stop, Hawaii, I was ready to throw caution to the wind. I joined my friends on the top deck, lining up our lounge chairs, with mine in the center. I was given the prime location for my cheered rebellious sunbathing. I had such fun that last week—returning to my room at the end of the day and quickly showering, hoping I would be a few shades lighter after a rigorous soaping. In hindsight, I'm sad for that younger Aparna. Why end such a glorious day with that thought?

Well, because I am Indian. And I was told that the deep brown of my arms was not desirable. This is the heaviness we grow up with, even when we live in the United States and are given amazing educations at prestigious universities, even when we travel the world and have assorted friends who are not South Asian like us. Who is this "we"? The South Asian girl living in a world where she learns to keep her skin as fair as possible, to control what is otherwise just a part of nature and the human body doing its work. "We" are not immune from these pressures to be "fair and lovely," even if we are given independence to grow and thrive in all other areas of our life. But in those weeks leading up to my disembarkation back to reality, I lived on my own terms. And I loved it. By the time we got to Hawaii, I had embraced the sun worshipping of my friend group. I joined them for a full day on Waikiki Beach. After kissing American soil and eating cheeseburgers, we headed to an open spot on the expansive yellow sand, no umbrella in sight, and I wasn't the least bit worried for once. I didn't need the shade. I stretched out my towel and lay down in the delicious warmth of the day. I napped off my French fries before dusting off the sand to go down to the ocean. Christmas music played from the far-off beach shacks as we lay on floaties in the water. I got back on that ship and spent the last few days doing more of the same on the once-elusive deck.

We docked in San Diego, and I flew home a few hours later. All my friends at Rice University cooed over my "gorgeous tan" and shared they enviously wished they had the same. My mother raised her eyebrow when I asked her to comment on my appearance. She refrained and asked, "So you had fun, right? That's good." But it was the winter holidays, and within a few days we were at a large gathering of South Asian friends. All the kids were home from college, and we separated from our parents so they could hear about all my adventures of living on a cruise ship. Before we could grab chairs and sit in the corner, one aunty stopped me in the kitchen to loudly announce, "Who will marry you now? You've become so dark." I was honestly mostly confused and fully stunned that this woman I know to be kind and full of humor, said *that*. I was twenty years old. I was not in the least bit worried about my future husband. I rationally mused, *Well, this tan will have long faded by the time I'm looking for a husband, Aunty.* I just saw the whole world, ten countries in one hundred days, circumnavigating the globe by sea. I felt like a Vasco de Gama of my generation, on a high from an experience I would never properly be able to put into words. And this aunty was worried about my marriage prospects. It didn't fit well, not then and not as I continued my studies.

Always curvy with baby-face cheeks, I was assured by my mom that my face would shed its youthful fullness in my late twenties, just like hers did. She was right. Throughout my schooling, from university to law school to the two study abroad experiences in Italy during that time, I relied on being confident, assertive, well-spoken, and "interesting." My mother and sister visited me for two weeks when I lived in Florence during my senior year of college. I showed them the city from the Arno River to Santa Maria Novella and beyond before whisking them off to Lucca, Venice, and then down south to the Amalfi Coast. Now I don't know if you know this about Italian men, and especially Italian servers, but they love the women traveling to their country in search of mouthwatering pizza, delicious Chianti wines, and yes, some Italian serenading. And serenade you they will! They passed over my sister and me (age twenty-two and twenty-four at that time) and went straight to my mother. Flourishing with outstretched arms, sometimes on their knees, always with a wink and a smile—these men were drawn straight to my laughing mother. Now to be fair, my mother had us when she was quite young, so she was only in her late forties at that time. And she was glowing.

I didn't mind, either. I was used to it by now. My whole life, men had held doors for my mother, stopped on the street to give her a smile, and bequeathed her with small tokens of their appreciation of her beauty. And I was always told I looked "just like my father," so I didn't think those gestures were reserved for me, not in my twenties and not for many years to come. This was just life. And in my life, mothers are beautiful well into their forties. They are youthful, well dressed, and always smell like a tuberoses with a slight tinge of powder. The only reality we ever know is the one we live, and in my reality I was genetically disadvantaged. So I was also then free. Perhaps I was "dark and short" at a whopping five foot three. Perhaps my mother did stand fair and tall at five foot seven. Perhaps my sister even favored my mother with her skin color and height. But that just meant the lesson I learned was even more valuable. I was allowed an opportunity by this genetic gamble that was not in my favor. I was given the chance to embrace every aspect of cosmetic nonconformance and to use it to develop myself more fully. I question, would I speak so clearly and confidently if I always had beauty to rely on? Would I storytell lessons of resilience and grit? Would I take chances to find love—real love, a partnership of a lifetime—if I was always assured I was worthy of a man who was "a catch"? I know the answer to those questions, and it's a resounding no.

So if you're wondering how to make your own story, independent of your family, separate from that of your beautiful mother (or sister, or cousin, or best friend), let me show you the emancipation that comes with just being uniquely yourself. Let me tell you of the liberties you're afforded by not being weighed down by traditional standards of beauty. Let me assure you that you are the lucky one who gets to grow, evolve, and most important, eliminate the people and situations that don't serve you. No one has set expectations for you based on where you "should and could" go because of your looks. So go forth and embrace the "ugly duckling" privilege. I sure have. And I'd have it no other way.

8

LEARN LESSONS FROM WOMEN BEFORE YOU

THERE IS NO NEED TO REINVENT the wheel. This is a saying that has guided my life. And do you know who invented the wheel? Women.

OK, maybe not literally. (We don't know if it was a woman who invented the wheel, although if you ask me, it's likely a woman did. Picture a potter in ancient Mesopotamia spinning a circular apparatus on an axis—it's ingenuous and clever and *of course* it would take a woman to come up with that.) But I also don't mean the literal wheel. I'm talking about life and its many—often winding—roads. Roads that women before you have navigated.

I am Sindhi, which means I am from a region called Sindh located in modern-day Pakistan. For hundreds—if not thousands—of years, my family owned vast amounts of property and thrived as *zameendaars* (landowners) in this area. Until one day—August 14, 1947, to be exact—the country of Pakistan (formally known as the Islamic Republic of Pakistan) was created from the Partition of India. With interreligious violence erupting throughout Karachi, my family was forced to flee in the middle of the night as throngs of angry mobs circled their house and banged at the gates with lit torches in their hands. My great-grandmother,

great-grandfather, and several of their children, including my
grandfather, left their home escorted through the back entrance
by a friendly high-government official.* They were whisked to a
jailhouse, in the hopes of keeping them safe overnight. It worked.
In the morning, a chartered plane flew them to Bombay.

The only possessions they had upon arriving in India were
basic household items packed quickly by the low-level government officials who returned to the *haveli* (traditional mansion)
overnight, as well as any jewelry hastily thrown on their bodies
before leaving. Amma, my paternal great-grandmother, was in
her thirties when she arrived in Bombay. I can only imagine her
fear and confusion, settling into an unfamiliar place after leaving
the only home she ever knew.

Still, she did not let fear paralyze her.

Using her jewelry, specifically three strands of Colombian
emeralds, Amma had the men in the family purchase a government contract to install electrical poles along the highway of Goa.
The Indian government was giving out these contracts to displaced
people who formerly resided in the region that had just been
named and drawn as Pakistan. It was supposed to be an opportunity for the families who moved involuntarily to India to gain
financial status, as well as to aid the newly independent India in
growing its infrastructure. Sadly, though, the local political chaos
kept them from meeting the project's deadlines. My family lost
everything in that failure. Amma had taken a risk—she'd wanted
to modernize her new, unfamiliar home and gain monetary stability for her family—and that risk failed. The disappointment
must have been crushing. She went from once having everything
to literally being left penniless.

---

* A few of my grandfather's siblings were traveling and were saved
from this fate.

But Amma was not crushed. With nothing to their name, my great-grandmother held the family together by selling pieces of jewelry to feed them and to secure basic shelter. Even in the most trying of times, she maintained grace and patience. Her sons would go off into the world to try to make their own way—my grandfather first going to Ghana, then Italy, Spain, and finally settling in Nigeria to make his fortune. Throughout it all, Amma was their anchor, their rock. Their home, always.

My great-grandmother's fortitude was the glue that rebuilt the family.

My grandfather took his bride to Spain at first, this bride being my maternal grandmother—in Hindi, Nani. They would quickly move to southeast Nigeria where my grandfather set up some of the first grocery stores in the Cross River State. When the Biafra Civil War broke out in 1964, Nani took it upon herself to send her two eldest children—my mother (age four) and her brother, Mahesh (age six)—to boarding school in India. With the country in turmoil, Nani saw it as the only way to guarantee a stable education for her children. That stability came with a price: at age four, my mother was alone and separated from her brother. Holidays were the only time they'd reunite, and even that was infrequent since Nigeria was so hard to access by plane in the 1960s and '70s. Many holidays were spent in Bombay, and often years would go by without my mother seeing her parents.

Nani saw education as a priority, though during family discussions some questioned the sacrifice of sending children abroad and the price paid for her ambition. And she was very ambitious. When my uncle turned sixteen, Nani knew she had to get him into Cambridge, which her own grandfather had attended generations prior. They'd lost their home and, with it, countless rituals and traditions—Nani was not about to let this tradition be lost as well.

Armed with only her eighth-grade education and two round-trip tickets, she arrived in London with my uncle in tow with the sole purpose of getting him admitted into one of the top feeder high schools to the elite universities of England. Staying in a small bed-and-breakfast near Paddington Station, she went to Gabbitas, an educational consultancy trust, for advice and insight into the top ten public schools in England. The goal was for my uncle to do his A-levels there and then go on to Cambridge.

Nani was all but told she was delusional.

It would be nearly impossible for him to get into any of the prep schools, they informed her with barely disguised condescending smiles. Children were placed on waitlists *from birth*. They looked down on Nani's lack of education—who was this deranged foreign woman who expected her son to be admitted into schools with the local upper class? But Nani was not deterred. She proceeded to go from school to school on the British Rail to meet with admissions officers in person. She knew how persuasive she could be. She was going to find a way for my uncle to be admitted into one of the top prep schools. Cambridge was his destiny.

In the end, my uncle received not one but two offers from prep schools.

By the end of his first year, he tested into Cambridge University. He was admitted for the following school year.

I grew up hearing this story from various family members. From an early age, I'd picture Nani and her no-nonsense posture—shoulders set, back straight—and be filled with pride. Nani was undaunted by the naysayers, undisturbed by her own lack of education. She would not stand for those who said it couldn't be done. My grandmother knew what she wanted, and if she had to go across the world to knock on doors, negotiating from school to school, all to secure her son's entrance, then she was going to do just that.

Nani never gave up. That is how she navigated life.

Which is why I've tried to navigate my life in the same way. When I hear a no, big or small, I don't take it. Because of Nani, I believe I can achieve what others deem impossible or unworthy of me. I hold firm to the certainty that I can—and will—get what I want. I, too, can change my own destiny and potentially that of my children one day. Of course I can.

Determination runs in my family. Nani proved that time and again.

And not just Nani.

My own mother took Nani's lesson one step further—maybe even one hundred steps further. In 1992, my mom did what so few South Asian women did: she left. Stuck in an unhappy marriage with nothing to her name except the jewelry her parents had given her on her wedding day eleven years before, my mom took her two kids—and her will to survive—across the world. She could not stay a moment longer, not in a society and a house where her every movement was controlled, tracked, and measured. I knew, even at the age of six, which is how old I was when we left, that my father had a temper. The walls in my house were thick, but not thick enough to contain the muffled yells, the loud thuds. My mother wasn't safe inside our home. She certainly wasn't happy. Happiness was nowhere to be found outside our house, either. We lived in an expatriate society where women gossiped endlessly in kitty parties, had no college education, and whiled away their time with dinners and shopping. Somewhere between the petty discourse and trivial dramatics, my mother feared losing herself. And so we left Dubai with two suitcases each.

We landed in Manhattan on March 20, 1992.

My sister's ninth birthday was the next day. When asked what she wanted to do to celebrate, she said, "I want to go to the top of the Empire State Building." So that's what we did. Picture us atop the iconic structure in the frigid cold wearing matching plaid wool coats. We felt like we were flying. Was my mom crumbling on the inside? Was she second-guessing her decision? If so, she never let on. That day, she took in the dimming, late-winter skyline, grinning along with us.

Years later, whenever I walk by that building, I smile as I remember the wind that whipped our hair out from under our hoods and the biting cold that seemed to freeze our toes. A true immigrant moment. Not quite the cinematic story of *Sleepless in Seattle* or *Love Story*, but a beautiful memory of one girl who dragged her newly immigrated family to the top of the world to celebrate a new life.

Now, mind you, life was not rosy. Nor was it sweet. In fact, hell came. High water came. But that did not dissuade my mother from believing she made the right choice in divorcing my father. After finding out we could not get into any private schools in New York, we enrolled in public schools in New Jersey. Our handyman robbed us—he took everything of value in the house, including a sizeable chunk of my mother's fine jewelry that wasn't in the bank's safety deposit box. We weathered the coldest winter in the books—after years of living in Dubai, that was brutal in its own right. Money became tight as our initial funds ran low, so my mother started her own stationery business and navigated through New York City with her ability to sell her beautiful wares to boutiques and museum gift shops. New York was tough. But so was my mom.

Eventually, she relocated us to Houston, where the weather was warmer, family lived nearby, and the public schools were excellent. And, just like that, Houston became home. My mom made it that way—safe, stable, comforting. We lived in a small city inside Houston city limits, a bubble where pharmacists knew your name and the same cops that taught you D.A.R.E. in third grade gave you your first ticket when you started driving and didn't heed the school zone signs. Life was ideal in this protected bubble she provided us. My friend group was diverse. I spent my elementary school years learning about Texan-based Native American tribes and attending Vietnamese friends' birthday parties. My Gifted and Talented program in middle school presented me with twenty-six bar and bat mitzvahs and ample opportunity to learn about students living all over the massive city of Houston—not just those in Bellaire.

My high school was large, bigger than my private university would be once I graduated. I learned to hone my own creativity in complex, college-level art history classes. I challenged myself in competitive geography teams (yes, that's a thing). I fed my love of stories by becoming the editor of my school newspaper. And through it all, I watched my mother work hard—the hardest I've ever seen anyone work. She transitioned through businesses she started, which would thrive or sometimes fail. Fashion. Stationery. Custom home building. Supplements. My mother never gave up. She hustled. And when she needed to, she picked up and moved on to the next endeavor. She didn't allow past failures to interfere with her future successes.

That mentality, that onward-and-upward approach, stuck with me. In my academic life, which often involved challenges that were deemed too much for me. In the businesses I started, which were often knocked down by life's unpredictability. In my constant search for love, when only the wrong men lined up in front of me.

If my grandmother taught me never to give up, it was my mother who taught me not to be afraid of failure. She'd failed, after all. In those days, leaving a marriage was considered a massive failure. Still, that failure allowed her to live life on her own terms. Her decision to leave my father—and all the security and comforts of wealth—granted her freedom. Freedom to want. To live. To be happy. That's another lesson my mom taught me: to value freedom. Because in coming to the United States, my mom secured my freedom as well. She ensured that I too would get to live life on my own terms: access to a great education, the choice to pick my own partner whenever the time was right for me, and the ability to travel the world. These are not things I take for granted. My life's story could've easily been different if not for my mother's bravery.

Independent. She allowed me that, always. All my life, I heard that word associated with myself. From my nannies who knew I would always be choosing my own clothes and having opinions about hair bows at age three, to aunties with their wagging tongues as I traipsed around the world. Even from the men I dated, who knew I didn't need to be cosseted when out together in public. I was encouraged to choose my own college—and major. I was encouraged to continue my education with an advanced degree and select whichever school made me *happy.* This was often criticized. South Asian mothers were supposed to urge their children to adhere to tradition, not value freedom and happiness.

But my mother paid no heed to the critics.

Instead, she applauded my willfulness, my strong sense of self. As a result, I paid no heed to the critics either. In fact, for the longest time, I paid no attention to any third person who had an opinion about my choices or less-than-traditional lifestyle. They didn't have to like me or my choices. *I* liked me. *I* liked my choices. For the most part, people seemed to pick up on that and left me (mostly) to my own devices.

Or they did—until I turned twenty-five.

Halfway through my twenties, that's when the incessant prodding began. At engagement parties, the teasing by clusters of aunties that *the time had come* and the well-intentioned comments from my friends to *keep an eye out for the right guy.* This was no arbitrary age. I'd just I graduated from law school, which, to my family, was code for *is ready for marriage.*

Except *I* wasn't ready. I wasn't anywhere near ready.

Marriage was something I could figure out later. It wasn't on my radar.

And then came the weddings. Extravagant, joyful, and big—the stream of huge Bollywood weddings invaded my life. Somehow everyone I knew was tying the knot. Here's the thing about Indian weddings: it's impossible to attend one and not hope for your own. The celebrations I witnessed got me daydreaming of my own big day. I'd picture my groom coming down the street on his white horse with his *baraat* (crowds of family and friends) in tow to meet me. I could see us at the *mandap*, the traditional Hindu altar, as we took those symbolic seven circles around the fire, thus making us husband and wife.

Here's what I couldn't see: the groom's face. Or any part of my life *after* the sure-to-be travel extravaganza of my dream honeymoon.

You see, the truth was that I wasn't ready at twenty-five. With the clarity of hindsight, I was likely not ready at thirty either. But no one would allow for that reality, because thirty was the age you invariably imploded if you were still unmarried. As a South Asian woman, thirty was also the age that you might even fall off a cliff, never to be seen again, if you hadn't yet lined up your groom. But coming off a chaotic seven years of undergrad and grad school and lining up my first job in the equally crazy recession years of 2009–2010, I needed to figure out life. Life *without* a partner. Life that allowed me time to learn about myself.

When I was twenty-eight, I spoke to an astrologer, a woman who warned me to wait to get married because I would lose myself in a marriage if I entered into one too soon. I didn't have it in me to grow independently within a relationship, she added.

Naturally, I scoffed at her prediction. I wasn't some easily led automaton! I was a strong, independent woman. But there was a part of me that was fearful too. A part of me that remembered how my own mother had nearly been lost forever to a horrible marriage. What if the same thing happened to me?

In response, the astrologer added, "And anyway, you won't be getting married until after the age of thirty-four."

That, more than anything, seemed impossible to me. Not even implausible. It was downright *never gonna happen*. I didn't crave a traditional lifestyle, but being thirty-four and unmarried seemed like a dire fate. (Oh, to be twenty-eight and strong and independent!)

The astrologer finished by announcing that I'd have sons, multiple sons. Twins.

Is she right? That's the question that would stir in the back of my mind for years to come.

Which is why when the *Indian Matchmaking* production team asked me if I wanted to meet with an astrologer, I readily agreed. This was an opportunity to see if another person would echo my first reading. By then I was—you guessed it—thirty-four. Would he say that now was the time for me to get married?

For the record, I'm not sure I believe in the accuracy of it all: astrology and planetary alignments and readings. But I also haven't ruled out that these charts tell a story of an individual's life. How could I, when I grew up listening to tales that depicted fate and karma and the power of predetermination in the stars? I'd been taught that it was tradition for your paternal grandmother to stand in the room when your mother was delivering so that someone was watching the clock and could record the exact moment of your birth. This information was important—it would be read to determine your future. For the longest time, I saw it as mere superstition. But maybe I was being too pragmatic. Or perhaps it was a case of self-fulfilling prophecy: the events forecasted only prove true because of the constant harping on their coming throughout the person's life. A classic chicken-or-the-egg situation. Did life happen because it was so written in the stars? Or did the stars, or in this case, the reading of the stars, dictate what happened?

Confession: I didn't know what to think. I didn't know what to believe.

At the end of the day, I thought *why not?*

I decided to go ahead and sit down with Dilip Uncle, an aeronautical engineer at Boeing in Los Angeles who moonlit as a *pandit* (a priest who marries couples) and an astrologer. He was told I was born in London, England, on January 4, 1985, at 1:48 PM. His computer software lined up the stars at that very moment in London. (I wonder, did the software know it was snowing that day and that, as my mom looked out the window, she saw a red post office box blanketed in snow and thought, *This is all a dream?*) I sat in front of him, the microphone on my back pinching my left shoulder blade, and waited.

On camera, he laughed and said, "Well it's clear. You were not going to get married until now. Your window for marriage is now, after age thirty-four . . . and by the way, twin boys. You're going to have twin boys."

I was dumbfounded. The prior reader had said the same thing. Thirty-four. Twins.

How did he know?

I peered at the circle filled with two-letter character combinations. How did *that* tell him all of *this?* He spoke to me at length about planets and alignment and then asked if I had any questions.

Of course, I had questions. (When have I not had questions in my life?)

Nervously, I looked around. The cameras were still on, but this was my only shot.

"Will I need IVF?" I asked.

He laughed. He told me I would not. While that concept is not traditional or age-old enough to be in the readings of birth charts, Dilip Uncle assured me I had no reproductive health issues. According to him, charts can read miscarriages or trouble conceiving. I had none of those issues.

I had one more question, "When will I be widowed?"

He sat back, slightly aghast but likely too polite to express it outright. "Why do you ask that?"

Curiosity, I claimed. I did not add that I knew I was meeting my husband later in life and, being in my thirties already, I just wanted to know how many years we would have together. It seemed silly to admit it, but what I wanted to know was *How long would my happily ever after last?*

Dilip Uncle looked down and chuckled. He seemed nervous. "Well, I don't know. I can't see that here. Why don't you find someone and then bring me his chart? Then I will be able to tell you."

I raised my right eyebrow. *Interesting*, I thought. He knew but he wouldn't tell me. I had no other questions.

Later that day, I thought back to our interaction. I relived the moment where I was sitting in front of cameras, asking an engineer if—really, *when*—I'd lose my husband one day. It was laughable, of course. I was there to find love. Why should I be focusing on how it will end?

But then I thought back to the past five years of mounting concern from friends and downright confusion from acquaintances. Why wasn't I looking more? Was I doing everything in my power to meet new people? Was I going to go alone to that wedding where I knew no one? Weddings are a good place to meet a single guy! Was I putting my best face forward on dating apps? I was interrogated over wine nights and girls' lunches. The clock was ticking. I had to know that, right? Right? RIGHT?

Right.

Is it any wonder I was afraid?

It's not that I didn't understand my friends' collective concern. I did. They saw their own lives moving forward happily with husbands and young children, and they wanted that for me too. I knew that, but I also couldn't change the fact that the endless parade of first dates was not resulting in me finding Mr. Right. I definitely wanted to find my partner, and while relationships would last a few months at times, no one was a good fit for me.

In my twenties, I gravitated toward emotionally unavailable men who were the life of the party: flashy and overly generous. My first heartbreak at age twenty-one was the president of two different clubs and the most charismatic charmer I had ever met. I was smitten by him. And when I realized he would never settle for one woman, let alone me, I hid under the covers and tried to shrink into the darkness of my dorm room.

On one of these rainy afternoons, my roommate came back early from class, gassed up the blender with frozen margaritas, and turned on TNT in the hopes I'd join her on the futon (and finally leave my bed). Diane Lane was on the screen in *Under the Tuscan Sun*. We watched as her husband left her, as she took a tour of Italy, and as she stayed there to heal. It hit me! Travel— my first love. That's what I needed. I would go to Italy. Just like Diane Lane, I would end up in an orange sundress in a field of sunflowers with a gorgeous new man.

I rushed straight to my study abroad office. Remember Chipmunk from my yearlong Semester at Sea appeal? She was still there. And now, in the fall semester of my senior year, she was surprised to see me again. This time, however, I wasn't looking for a ship. I wanted to go to Florence.

With ease and very little effort, I was signed up for a semester in Italy. It would be my last semester at Rice University, but

FOMO no longer gripped me. Instead, I just wanted out and far, far away from the playboy who broke my heart. So off I went, to an imagined place of sunshine and fields of flowers. Very little research prior to my spring semester abroad would have told me Florence is actually quite cold—frigid, in fact. I was met with gray skies and cold cobblestone streets when I arrived in January 2007. But it didn't matter to me. At least I was an ocean away from the reason for my endless tears. And they were certainly endless.

Since I didn't need the school credit to graduate (I had already completed my credits—consider this a bonus semester), I chose classes purely because they piqued my interest. Learning just for the sake of learning was an incredible privilege, and something I'd recommend to anyone. Thursdays became my favorite day of the week. That's when my Mediterranean cuisine class met, featuring nutrition majors from Boston University who cooked five-course meals as I sipped cooking wine in the corner. It was also when I attended wine-tasting seminars, where I learned obnoxious fac- toids about Super Tuscans and the best years for reserve Chiantis, knowledge I still use today. I skipped Italian class and still can only eke out a few words. Occasionally I popped in to creative writing, but mostly to write sappy memoir essays revolving around my broken heart. I was a mess.

Most days were spent wandering the streets with my pink mini iPod clipped to my jeans pockets, my headphones blaring James Blunt's "Goodbye My Lover" on repeat. I ate. I prayed. I loved—well honestly, the only things I loved were gelato, pasta, and wine. Despite walking miles each day, I gained twelve pounds. I would "rest" in the arches of the Ponte Vecchio bridge, crying into the Arno River below me as honeymooners snapped mem- ories on digital cameras and tried to avoid my downtrodden, curled-up self. To this day, I wonder if a sad, lonely Aparna is in the background of someone's framed memento from Florence.

Looking back, this makes me laugh. But there's also a part of me that hurts for the twenty-one-year-old who thought she'd never survive that searing pain.

Of course, I survived. But the men who came after always mimicked this first love—boisterous, extroverted overachievers who looked and sounded a lot like me. And sometimes, they wanted nothing to do with me. When I was younger, that sort of man often wanted the trophy girlfriend—not the well-rounded, driven female version of themselves. I dated a fair share of those men. I was rejected by a few too. It was a never-ending cycle of failures and beginnings.

In my thirties, watching my friends in their fulfilling marriages, I decided I wanted a man more like the ones they married—introverted, laid-back, happy to go with the flow but also comfortable asserting their opinions. Men who were intelligent and stable, and also kind and empathetic. It took me a full decade to figure out that these men were the treasures. Finally, in my thirties, I was ready for a genuinely good partner. Just as I'd been told—or maybe *because* I was told.

Except being ready didn't translate to finding someone. And not just for me.

I have a group of non–South Asian friends who are single. In my bluest moments, they continuously assure me that the right guy for me is out there and will come in due time. This group is large, diverse in geography and professions. These individuals are smarter than most of my other friends, more accomplished, better looking—they have everything going for them, or that's the way it appears to me. Yet they are single. Which is, in an odd way, comforting. I see their existence as proof that yes, sometimes good people just haven't met the partner for them ... yet. The timing involved in finding one's partner isn't about money (several of them have money) or looks (quite a few are *Vogue*-cover worthy).

It's fate or luck or timing or something else—something unnamed and uncontrollable. If you're single, it's very important to have single friends. Or else you will inevitably believe the problem is you.

To be clear: I wasn't passive about finding the right person. I knew I had to do the work, to put myself out there. I knew of so many people who spent their evenings alone in their apartments, turning down invitations from their friends to go out, logged out of dating apps—and yet, somehow, they expected to meet their partner. I was not going to be one of those people.

That's when the online dating began in fast and furious spurts. Two dates in one night, always during the week. I was unfailingly honest. If a man suggested a second date and I wasn't interested, I'd refuse point-blank. No ghosting. No letting things fizzle. I had no time to waste, so it was only fair that I not waste anyone else's time, either. I still got hurt—my system's efficiency did not grant me immunity to heartbreak.

A confession: I was still quite drawn to some of those "life of the party" guys of my past—often disappointed and defeated that I couldn't hold their interest and blaming myself for not being entertaining enough, pretty enough, or dumb enough to keep them around. These rejections hurt. But I carried on. After all, I was also doing some of the rejecting myself, though I did try to be kind when turning someone down. In fact, if I was on a date and felt the man was not right for me but was right for one of my single girlfriends, I would later text him asking if he would like to be set up with her. In fact, I saved this template to my iPhone's Notes app:

> In the spirit of online dating, it was wonderful meeting you but I don't think we have potential to go further than a friendship. I did like that you [were a vegetarian, a runner, from a certain community etc.] and believe you would

really be a good for my friend. She is [a vegetarian, a runner, from your same community etc.]. Would you be up for me connecting you two?

Most of the time, they'd say yes.

While none of these couples ended up staying together long-term, I fancied myself a modern-day matchmaker—a single woman keeping her eye out for her own match, as well as her friends' matches. Pragmatic and romantic—a romantic pragmatist! Efficiency and love-seeking all in one.

And that's how I expected my experience on *Indian Matchmaking* to be. For me, the show was a new avenue to meet my future partner. After all, who's to say where their meet-cute will take place? It could happen at the produce section of a grocery store. The singles' table at a wedding. A blind date set up by a friend. Or . . . through a matchmaker. Why not? If I wanted love, I had to go out and find it.

And now, another confession: *Indian Matchmaking* was not my first experience with a matchmaker.

Many years ago, after a particularly brutal breakup with Mr. So Wrong, I'd approached a South Asian matchmaker in Washington, DC. I was twenty-seven, and it was a time in my life when I had momentarily lost faith in my own judgment. I can recall the moment with perfect clarity: I was on a plane, nibbling on a cold sandwich and thumbing through a magazine I pulled out from the depths of my tote bag, when I came across an article about an American-born South Asian lawyer who couldn't find her own match years prior and thus opened her own matchmaking business for successful US-based clients like herself. I remember thinking to myself, *This is it. This is how I'll find my person.* For a brief, glorious moment, the pathway to my future husband was bright.

Except she refused me as a client.

After spending upward of $300 on a consult with her, this matchmaker wrote an email explaining that I was "too young" for her database and advising that I should try online dating. At the time—2013—I was horrified at her advice. Back then, online dating was relegated to websites like Match and eHarmony. Tinder had only recently hit the mainstream markets, and "girls like me" did not sign up for a service aimed at casual relationships. (Oh, how the world would change. The world and me.)

Not one to give up (thanks, Nani), I began my campaign to convince the matchmaker to take me on as a client. I wouldn't take no for an answer, which is something she probably picked up on because, finally, I talked her into taking my money ($10,000) for the retainer fee. But before I wrote the check, my mom sat me down and persuaded me to listen to the expert's advice. My tenacity was admirable, but if the matchmaker didn't think *she* was a fit for *me*, I should respect her opinion.

I listened to my mom. And she was right. (Thanks, Mom.)

The lesson: if someone is telling you they're not for you, don't try to change their mind. Whether that's a matchmaker or a prospective boyfriend, their opinion matters and should hold the weight of truth. Maya Angelou once spoke to Oprah about her famed quote, "When someone shows you who they are, believe them." She went on to remind Oprah, "And when someone tells you who they are, you better believe them!"

A streak of acceptance sat right with me. We were all looking for something. For love. For a matchmaker. And I didn't know where I'd find either of these. But I understood it wouldn't be with someone who was telling me they weren't for me. That was the day I stopped taking rejections from men personally. If I just wasn't "enough" for a man as I was, then I still had a duty to myself to say, *I like me. I like the woman I am today and the woman I am trying to grow into tomorrow.*

Looking back, I can see how this experience shaped my outlook on dating. It helped me understand that a man's role in my life was to be my *partner*. Not my *boyfriend* and then later *my husband.* But a true partner—a teammate, someone who would stand by my side through the hard times and the good, my cheerleader and my support system. I would be a partner to him in the same right. It was a two-way street. He had to want me as much as I wanted him.

Years later, I did find a matchmaker—one who happily agreed to take me on as a client. It happened when I was ready. I remember sharing these stories with the show's production team. They prompted me in one of my on-screen master interviews—the one I would do from my couch in my orange dress—to tell the world why I was going on *Indian Matchmaking.* I remember telling them about this epiphany as the cameras rolled. I used the two-way street analogy. I thought it would be easy for them to understand. I wanted love not only because I wanted to be loved. I also wanted love because I wanted to *give* love. Cheesy, but true.

But that explanation never made it to the screen, even though it was certainly taped.

Instead, I was the uncompromising, stubborn shrew.

I get it. Enough time has gone by that I really do get it. *Indian Matchmaking* called itself a reality show, but it wasn't grounded in reality. The reality is that I am a person. In the show, I was character. Characters have to fit an archetype. They have to follow an arc.

Still, it was confusing for me to watch myself acting like . . . well, *not* like myself.

Yes, it's true that I said, "I will have to say to my partner, sorry, some parts of me are done." They included that in the show. But they didn't include what I said next, which was, "And I assume there are parts of them that I will have to accept. We are after all meeting as developed adults."

Is that pickiness? Aren't we *supposed* to be discerning with the one member of our family that we get to choose? After all, we don't choose our parents, siblings, or even our own children. I would like to think that my future partner would be equally as picky when choosing his partner. I certainly don't want someone who settled for me. I want someone who has been looking for me for years, just as I have been looking for him. Like I said: two-way street.

Unlike most of my friends, I did not get the benefit of meeting my partner in my teens or twenties. I will meet my future husband as an adult woman—one who is formed with many of her opinions and viewpoints on the world. My political leanings. The way I approach my relationship with my family. My health and wellness choices. My interests outside of work. The lessons I've learned from the women before me. I am a full person. Had I met this same man at age nineteen, I might be an entirely different person. I don't like that I still haven't found love. But I do appreciate how years of being single allowed me to be with myself. To make myself. And I like how I made myself. I'm protective of that.

For now, I'm still learning how to be OK with my single status. It helps to focus on all that it's given me, all that it's allowed me to do. Travel the world. Remain so connected to my family. Be a devoted friend. Start a business on a whim. Learn to rely on myself.

It's not all good. Of course not. But it's not all bad, either.

Indian Matchmaking simplified me into an archetype. The viewers gobbled up this woman, and many spat her straight out. I was the "Independent Woman" to them. Someone without the pangs of wanting a partner. A woman who was disdainful of men and closed off to the idea of bending her life to fit into a partnership. That is certainly not the woman I am—but then again, no one is such an easy, simple archetype. We are all more complex as individuals. However, showing those individuals with such nuance wouldn't fit into eight episodes, each only forty minutes long. Nor, more honestly, would those individuals' stories garner the worldwide attention seen when people are made into characters for eliciting strong reactions, and, of course, much-desired ratings.

In a strange way, I am thankful to have gone through the process of being viewed as Aparna-the-character. Not because I identify with her—I don't. But because it's taught me so much about myself. It's taught me to own my independence. To own my strength. To be proud of being in charge of my own destiny.

Difficult. Picky. These words are not meant as compliments.

But I take them as precisely that.

No, I will not succumb to societal norms because it's easier. No, I will not settle for a man who requires me to dim myself. I will not be tamed. Because I am my mother's daughter. I am Nani's granddaughter. I am Amma's great-granddaughter. I have been brought up under their wisdom. I have learned from their independence and strength, their fortitude and grit.

Without their lessons, I would not be me. And that to me is just not acceptable.

I very much hope that a partner will come when the time is right. But in the interim, I will still learn, grow, and reach for new heights. Even if that means I am doing it alone.

9

BODY-BUILD YOUR MUSCLE
CALLED RESILIENCE

WHAT MAKES SOME PEOPLE STRONGER THAN OTHERS? What makes them face challenges head-on? What allows them the fortitude to persevere, even when it seems the deck is stacked against them? It's resilience. Life events, especially the ones in which we are most uncomfortable, build a muscle called resilience.

My resilience building began at the age of sixteen. Sure, life happened before then, those little events like middle-school girl antics, the death of a grandparent, and the first mini heartbreak from a boy. But I'm talking life-altering events. We all have them. Some of us experience them at a young age. Some of us are protected for a while longer. But it happens to each one of us, and what we do with those moments is what makes us who we are. After all, life is a series of imperfect moments. I believe 90 percent of the outcome is our reaction to the event; the other 10 percent is the event itself.

I got sick when I was sixteen, the least sweet year of my life when it was allegedly going to be the sweetest. While my peers were planning their parties and lip gloss shades, I was in and out of doctors' officers. There was no diagnosis for seven long months. The not knowing was killing me, but it also felt like the sharp stomach pains, the constant vomiting, the ulcers that coated my mouth and throat, and the extreme fatigue might also kill me. It didn't; that's evident from where I sit today. But as doctors prodded me, examined every inch of my body, ran every battery of tests, I had not a moment nor an ounce of energy to be just sixteen. I only survived. That's all I could handle. The diagnosis of Crohn's disease came on September 11, 2001. As the first plane struck the World Trade Center, I sat in a pediatric gastroenterologist's office. She came in shaking, my colonoscopy results in her hands. My head was between my knees as I fought back the constant urge to vomit. I couldn't even comprehend what she was saying when she told us a second plane had hit the towers. I was in pain. I was nauseous. I was handed a diagnosis of a chronic condition with no cure and no known cause. The only solution was high doses of steroids that would start immediately. The world was falling apart, quite literally that day. And my small world did too.

I was handed pamphlets on this autoimmune condition to take home. The office would be closing that day. The Texas Medical Center was suspected to be the next target. It was being evacuated. My mother and I left, clutching the pastel literature and trying to quickly get home.

The steroids wreaked havoc on my body, the side effects ranging from intense weight gain to the "moon face" associated with the drug to losing my hair in clumps. The year was filled with undergoing invasive procedures and being constantly probed by doctors. Insomnia from the steroids took over, even while my body was exhausted from trying to heal. I was in and out of school for months and lost all my so-called friends. They did not want to deal with me, and at the time, I was resigned to that fact. (Now, I am horrified that children are so callous, and my mother recently shared she was saddened to see the lack of empathy in those "friends.") It turns out long-term chronic conditions are not conducive to being a "cool" sixteen-year-old. As others got their driver's licenses, I struggled to keep afloat. My only focus was to keep going through each day. I developed what I call my *survival mode.*

And to survive, I had to think long-term. This is an unusual skill for a teenager, who is usually barely concerned with the week ahead of her. But I knew that my macro planning would have to start now to ensure that my future could stay intact. My future was supposed to include moving to the Northeast to attend an Ivy League college, preferably Columbia or Harvard. I knew my grades had to be impeccable, that I had to take college-level classes for a majority of my curriculum, and that there was no margin for error. Even if that error was a chronic autoimmune disease. I convinced myself the universities would not care about those plights and would dismiss me if I did not have a high grade point average, lots of extracurricular activities, and a retail job to show my commitment to fiscal responsibility. In an era of university admissions frowning upon privilege, our college counselors at school told us to prioritize "relatability"—a.k.a. working for minimum wage in a local store for a few hours a week. As an immigrant whose mother had not gone to college in the States, we took all this advice to heart, and then some. It became my playbook.

So as I struggled each day to get out of bed, muster the strength to make it through a school day, and somehow participate in "normal teenage life," I grew increasingly solutions-oriented. I learned how to turn off my feelings of defeat, despair, and overwhelming doubt. Quite simply, those feelings took too much energy away from me. And I was low on energy to begin with. So instead, I was laser-focused on solutions. Mini ones, a series of them that would get me through the day. I constantly asked myself, *Is this going to help you reach your goal? If no, then stop. Discard. Move on.* With my body effectively breaking down, there was so much I could not control. But I could control my high grade point average. In between stints at home with extreme flare-ups, I would coordinate notes from classmates and nap all day with alarms set every two hours to wake up and read textbooks. Kind teachers offered for me to simply not take tests, but instead I begged for at-home test taking to not fall behind. Every part of the curriculum was taught for the ultimate standardized AP exam at the end of the school year. I knew if I didn't keep up with the syllabus, I would not pass the test. And then top universities would see those scores when I applied to school. I had my mind—even if my body was failing me.

This period of nine months passed in a blur, and as my medical team tweaked a sustainable health plan for me, I was able to return to a semblance of normal life. The swollen face, weight gain, and hair loss plagued me for months after, but otherwise, I was able to rejoin the teenage society whose biggest worry was the next party and whether that boy in chemistry class liked so-and-so and not you. I never fully rejoined mentally. I was always acutely aware that at any point my body could disappoint me again. At any point, I could be sick. While at first it was an effort, now, in my thirties, watching my body is a lifestyle. I am aware of foods that don't work, dips in energy, dark circles from fatigue caused by the Crohn's, and times when alcohol or coffee cannot be tolerated. Every day is a constant watch for symptoms that I might not be OK. I've spoken to others with autoimmune conditions and they've reported the same. Maintaining health is a part of your life. That's indeed the crux of living.

In my last year at my diverse and competitive high school, I started a new IV biological drug that is administered every eight weeks. It was only available in a few cities in the United States, and my doctor had an in to get me access to it. I asked what a biologic is, and I was told this one is a "perfect" blend of human and mouse DNA. I made a note to look it up one day but never did. This is a prime example of an interest that does not get addressed because it is extraneous to getting to the next step—a.k.a. admission into a great university. My family joked I was becoming more mouse-like by the day: cheese nibbling was a hobby, and my nose was always itchy from the allergies I developed now that my immune system was depressed from the drugs. I was able to balance my involvement in over ten different clubs, work a retail job in a boutique, and continue to take all college-level courses while maintaining an A average. I began the application process to my dream schools in the Northeast until my mother sat me down one day to deliver the bad news. I can't go. I can't leave Texas. I need to be within driving distance of the Houston hospital that administers my IV every eight weeks. All my doctors were in Houston, and it was too risky to move my carefully crafted health care infrastructure. She was right. I knew she was. But I was still devastated. I applied to Rice University, a top university in Houston, and was accepted under the Early Decision program. My fate was sealed.

I reluctantly started at Rice in the fall of 2003 with a strict agreement with my mother that I would live in the dorms there, even though Rice is three miles from my childhood home. Even though I could not go "away" to college like all my friends, I still wanted to feel a sense of independence and freedom. And sure enough, I did. I loved my experience in college. My health was under control with the IV medicines. I was well adjusted and happy with my classes. I explored extracurricular activities, from powderpuff football to theater to Bollywood dancing. I studied abroad for two semesters. And I had the most wonderful large and diverse group of friends—ranging from a Korean art major from Buffalo to a South Indian premed major from the Bay Area to a Quaker chemistry major from the Pacific Northwest. My world was filled with various ethnicities, and I enjoyed sharing in my friends' interests and backgrounds. I performed in a K-pop dance show, I visited a Quaker church for Sunday service, and I shared with friends microwaved *rasam* and rice that had been frozen and sent all the way from California. Life was ideal on this small, bubble-like campus. I was the happiest I've ever been.

Immediately following Rice University (and my semester in Florence), I started law school in Nashville in the fall of 2007. I picked Vanderbilt University Law School for its similarities to Rice. It was another small, southern private institution. A national ranking that polled "happiest universities" always had Rice at the top of the list. When that same magazine polled "happiest law schools," Vanderbilt made the list. I had never been to Tennessee, and I didn't get to visit law schools since I drank and cried my way through Florence in my last semester of college. So it was a blind pick based on the information I had in front of me, which in hindsight was minimal.

My mother and sister drove me from Houston to Nashville with a car full of my worldly belongings. They helped me buy and set up new furniture for my room. I had two wonderful room-mates—a bright, well-traveled fellow law student from Fort Wayne, Arkansas, and a local Nashville resident who was studying at Vanderbilt Nursing School. We lived in a three-bedroom apartment in a complex full of other graduate students from various Vanderbilt programs. And I settled in as best as I could in my new surroundings. On the night my mom and sister left, Jamie (my fellow law student roommate) invited me out with the other students in our program. Classes didn't start for a few days, and they had organized events for students to get to know each other before school was in session. I joined and quickly realized that Nashville would be my third study "abroad" after Semester at Sea and Florence, Italy. This place was like nothing I had ever seen before. Only well-versed in New York City, San Francisco, and Miami (while having briefly visited other American cities for short weekends), I had never fully experienced a city that was this . . . homogenous.

That night out was spent in honky-tonks with amazing live music. Thankfully, I had gone through a "country music phase" in high school with my sister, so I recognized some classics being played on stage. My new peers bopped to the beat and belted out every word to every song. I watched from the side of my eye as I tentatively sipped on beers and took well-intentioned celebratory rounds of lemon drop shots. What was I doing here? And what had I done by choosing to commit three years to this place? The night ended in a karaoke bar that was open from 2:00 AM to 5:00 AM. Those who were left were rambunctious and kind. All of us were twenty-two, straight from our universities' senior year partying lifestyle, and ready to continue that trend at this elite law school. They enveloped me into their world quickly, and I enjoyed the novelty of the experience while acutely aware of my outsider status.

———————

School starts and I realize, here, for the first time in my life, a predominantly White population surrounds me. Gone are the Asian, Indian, Black, Latin, and mixed-race friends of Rice and high school days. And not just in the city but in my school too. The small population of Black students keep to themselves a lot, joking loudly at their self-designated tables in the lobby. I envy them and their close ties to one another. There is one South Asian guy in my class and two women who are half-Indian and half-White. They identify more with the White side of their culture, it seems. There is no *rasam* to be shared here. The one guy ignores me completely so as to not associate with the one other South Asian. I quickly see how it's going to be.

It doesn't take long for me to experience the local blend of racism either. The law school is on the edge of a string of bars and restaurants. One day, a few days into the school year, Jamie and I are leaving class together to go our cars. We walk into the parking lot kitty-corner from our building. We had both parked there in the morning and now look at each other confused as we circle the lot. Neither of our cars are there. A second-year student comes up behind us, asking if our cars are gone too. We deduce that we had all parked along the back side of a bar. Three White men are loitering by the dumpsters of the bar just watching us as they spit their chewing tobacco to the ground. The 2L student, a Black man, asks them if they knew where our cars had been taken. They slit their eyes at him and move closer. With scorn in their voices, they tell us that *they* had them towed because the spots, although not marked, were reserved for clients of their establishment. Jamie and I instinctively move back, taking steps toward the center of the lot without turning. The male student walks toward them as a dark feeling of foreboding comes over me. The situation escalates within a minute. The student asks the men why they didn't just leave notes on our windshields this first week of school. He also asks why they didn't clearly mark the area as a no-parking zone for those not visiting the bar. The men get agitated, even though the student remains relatively calm.

They advance more, shouting slurs to the young Black man, telling him they will lynch him like they lynched his daddy. I am shaking and now in the corner of the parking lot, shielding myself partially by the dumpsters behind the bar. Jamie is frozen, watching them shove the student back and forth, his backpack zipper opening and his textbooks falling to the ground. I quickly pull out my phone, call 911, and whisper to the dispatcher that I'm scared. There are three White men screaming racial slurs and pushing our Black classmate around. The cops show up within minutes, quickly breaking up the scene and separating the men. The men give one last spit at the Black student even as the police move them inside their bar.

The cops come over to Jamie and me, inquiring which one of us called. They take our names and contact numbers so they can call us later for witness statements. This could potentially be considered a hate crime with the charge of assault against the three men who shoved our classmate. I'm in a daze. I go home and consider calling my family to tell them I want to come home. But I hold off. I need to process this. Was the incident a one-time rare occurrence, or was this place in the "deep old South" just not for me or anyone who looked like me?

As the story of the incident spreads through campus, students ask me how I'm doing. *I'm fine*, I tell them. *Ask the Black student. He was the one who was harassed and pushed around by those hateful men.* The dean of the law school calls me into his office that next day, his administrative assistant making the appointment on his behalf. An empathetic man, and also a Jew from New York, the dean inquires if I am OK and if I need some counseling or assistance in any way. He shares he has heard about the incident and assures me that this is not representative of Nashville as a whole. I am dubious. It's only a week into the semester, and I share with him that I am considering contacting other law schools to transfer to a more urban and diverse city. There is one that recently took me off its waitlist, just days prior. While I have declined the school's late admission already, I am now tempted to call back and beg for entrance into the school. The dean asks me to reconsider and again reassures me that Nashville is in fact a welcoming, diverse city. Still not sure, I tell him I appreciate his time and him checking up on me.

While I do end up staying, it's mostly because I can't face the thought of relocating with school already in session. It was hard enough to set up one apartment with shared roommates. I could not imagine doing it again with no notice. I resolve to face my time in Nashville like a study abroad program—a different universe from anything I've experienced before. I will enjoy the local fare (a series of southern comfort foods mixed with an array of bland soups, salads, and sandwiches). I will enjoy the nightlife, which consists of talented musicians on stage each night singing a genre I'll have to get more familiar with. I will learn the mannerisms, the norms, the style of dress. I start wearing ballet flats and discard my flip-flops from Texas living. Sweats and jeans are replaced with flouncy skirts and a wardrobe of sundresses. We tailgate for football games in the fall, the women all wearing dresses in Vanderbilt's colors of gold and black, while the men wear seersucker suits and bow ties. I order beers at the end of the nights out, like everyone else. I start inserting "Bless her heart" into any phrase that could be construed as mean-spirited. For example, *She's not the brightest crayon in the box . . . bless her heart. She's looking rough after last night's party . . . bless her heart.* It goes on and on. I get used to *bye* being four syllables (bah-ah-i-iye). I notice that southerners say, "oh my gah." When I ask why, I am told its because one shouldn't take the lord's name in vain. Truly, when compared to my world before this place, I am in a whole new country.

But I've grown that resilience, like I mentioned, and so over time I do what I can to find a solution to fit in. I partake in the activities everyone else enjoys, from football games to karaoke nights to Thursday night social activities cheekily named Bar Review. I even get a car that fits into the Nashville scene—a BMW 3 Series with a sun and moon roof that I open whenever I can. On the outside, I have assimilated. On the inside, I remain an outsider. As the years move on, my first year, then the second and the third, I am more aware that I do not fit in and that I cannot wait to get back "home" to where things are normal. Every summer, I revel in the diversity and culture of Houston and my friends there. Every fall, I return to school and have to relearn the culture of Nashville. It's a jarring contrast. By my third year at Vanderbilt, I schedule my classes into a concentrated two days a week so I can travel for five days of every week. I go either to Houston or to a different city to visit my friends from my "past life." I am checked out. I am tired of living in a foreign land where, sure, the people are lovely, but they're not my people. A few friends there are gems, people I consider true friends even today, fifteen years later. But most are individuals I know I will never see again, and in hindsight, I treated them accordingly.

———————

I look back now and realize that the isolation felt in those three years really cemented my desire to date and marry a South Asian man. The lack of community and likeness in that space left me yearning for a familiarity in my future life partner. For me, that person would crave dal and rice for dinner, understand that every friend of a parent was an "aunty" or "uncle," and have no qualms about yearly trips to Mumbai. This man would understand so many things I previously took for granted before moving to a city that was devoid of that same understanding. Men in Nashville thought they were complimenting me with pickup lines like "Has anyone told you that you look like Jasmine from *Aladdin*?" Or, "Wow, you're so *exotic*." Honestly, I knew rationally that these were well-intentioned young men, but I was unamused at being compared to a cartoon character that wasn't even Indian by origin. You might wonder what it looks like to be a lone fish out of water. As it turns out, a fish that can pretend to walk is a resilient fish. And this resilient fish finished out her years in Nashville with more resolve than ever to live on her own terms and within her own comfort zone.

Today, I have gained even more muscle called resilience through horrible workplaces that are demeaning to women of color like myself, through hurricanes that devastated my community and my own home, and through heartaches that took me across the world. I am fully prepared with all the tools I need to pick myself up when I am kicked in the gut by a harsh portrayal of my likeness on *Indian Matchmaking*. After I cry, scream, and am stonewalled when I ask for help, I start fighting back. Shekar brings it to my attention that there might be some insight I can gain from other women who claimed they were wrongfully vilified in television—ones who are clear in the media that they don't agree with their own portrayals on their respective shows. I DM a few and ask what their advice is for coping with these days and weeks post–show launch. Overwhelmingly, they tell me to turn off my phone, deactivate social media, and if possible, leave town. Their advice, without them saying it, is to cower and hide.

No way. I sit back at the end of these text conversations with more conviction than ever. Here I am, thirty-five years old at this point, mad, sad, and feeling absolutely obliterated on international television. I was not going to take this as my fate. I had not gone through every trial and tribulation in my life to allow them to tell my story. I would tell my own. I would do it for all of us. I have learned the most important lesson of all: we are never defined by life's imperfect moments. After all, life is 10 percent what happens to you and 90 percent how you react to it. I am overwhelmed with gratitude for my fortitude as I begin the long and arduous task of speaking my truth to whoever will listen. I lean fully into my resilience.

10

WAIT FOR THE GUY
WHO KNOWS BOLIVIA
HAS SALT FLATS

T HERE WAS A POINT when I didn't have a social calendar, only a
work one. By Friday afternoon, the calendar was blank and the
weekend was mine for fun and unscheduled socializing. Everyone
would gather for an end-of-week happy hour, usually on a rooftop
with bar bites and margaritas flowing (this is Houston, after all).
Saturdays were left for spending time with family, running errands,
or sometimes even another get-together for a wine festival or
holiday event. The "holiday" could range from the Kentucky Derby
to St. Patrick's Day, to be fair. *Festive* was a loose term. Sundays
were recovery days, consisting of sleeping in until 11:00 AM and
often making it to a brunch with another set of friends. Eggs benny
and mimosas flowing, this was the meal where we could discuss
the breakdown of the weekend's gossip. This was life in sleepy old
Houston, and I loved it.

Then the weddings started. First slowly, when I was about
twenty-five, but then fast and furious by the time I was twenty-
seven. More than half my friends are South Asian, so those weddings started on a Thursday with a "home event" for close friends,

moved on to a Friday night *sangeet*, a Saturday morning *baraat* (for the groom), and then the ceremony, followed by the Saturday night grand reception. Sundays were clearly for recovery. Non–South Asian weddings usually involved travel, so those weekends were spent zipping to Dallas, San Francisco, or New York to catch events there—the more traditional rehearsal dinners and then the next-day ceremony followed directly by a reception. They were much less involved than a Hindu wedding but equally as fun for me to attend. By age thirty, these wedding invites slowed down with only a few coming in from the late bloomers. And those coincided with the first of the baby showers.

Suddenly I had a social calendar, and it was filled with baby showers, first birthday parties, and "sip and sees." Have you heard of a sip and see? It's a way for a couple to decline requests from friends to see the baby in the hospital or at the home. They can point to the sip and see event, where you sip on mimosas and see the baby, as a time for you to meet the little one for the first time. It's prevalent in the South where drawing boundaries often gets obfuscated into throwing a party. It allows the couple to spend time with their baby, often their first, and deal with the ups and downs of that period in peace. The sip and see happens after the child's first round of vaccines. It gives parents a polite excuse to wait the first forty days without visitors. I fully approve of this event, of course. I also attended a lot of these events. Saturday morning became a baby shower at so-and-so's mother-in-law's house, and Saturday afternoon was shuttling over to a sip and see (often with the same morning crowd) and then collapsing at home after throwing off the floral dress and strappy heels. It was repetitive. It was boring. And it felt never-ending. I'm happy for my friends. They are exactly where they "should" be: married by thirty, first child by thirty-two, second by thirty-four or thirty-five, and children's birthday parties galore. I was invited to most of the first birthday parties, fewer second birthday parties, and almost no third birthday parties.

My friends, all of them moms, see each other at those events and properly catch up with a child on one hip and another running on the playground. They do not go out at night, understandably exhausted from the weekend daytime activities and from a lack of childcare. That means I often don't go out at night, since they make up the majority of my friend group.

I join the Junior League of Houston, a philanthropic volunteer organization in Houston with a strong history of service and networking for the women initiated into its ranks. Its membership involves members paying dues and then giving approximately seventy-five hours of their time per year to a local organization as a volunteer. I join to meet new women, and I am pleased to open my social circle to a group that is outside my friends from college. Many of these women at the Junior League are transplants to Houston, a city that is not the easiest to navigate for those who do not have a familial or social setup already in place. They are friendly and outgoing, and I form strong friendships with them and happily fill my newly opened weekends with spa days, champagne brunches, and cookouts at someone's pool. It's notably not a South Asian crowd, and I enjoy meeting women with such varied backgrounds. Some are divorced, some unmarried in their thirties like me, and all are go-getter, be-involved kind of people. That's what made them sign up for an organization that requires so much of their time. I still see my old friend group, but a lot less frequently. Now my life has more frilly tea parties, and the baby showers are replaced by Saturday morning volunteering at Dress for Success, an organization that helps women from disadvantaged backgrounds prepare for their first interviews. I help style them with their first complimentary suit, shoes, and handbag. I assist in teaching them interview skills, ranging from preparing short pitch statements to ensuring they are ten minutes early for their interview (not more and not less, for purposes of etiquette).

I'm also growing increasingly unhappy with my work—not just the toxic office I work in but the profession as a whole. Each job, and I held five over the course of ten years, was more miserable than the last. Politics abounded, management was often sexist and/or racist, and the billable hour ran my life. I had to find a way out. And for me, it wasn't going to be a husband and a baby. Although I did want that for myself, the men I was meeting just didn't gel with what I wanted in my future life partner. They were nice, fine, OK. But they weren't for *me*. I worried out loud to my closest friends. Time was ticking and I was moving into my mid-thirties. Thirty-three was not a good number, we decided, and neither was thirty-four. All of us decided that my participation in the "Netflix show" made sense. After all, wouldn't it be the sweetest meet-cute if I found my future partner on a TV show? It would explain why it took me so long to find someone to begin with. It would be the *why* we were all looking for.

I started taping the show when I was thirty-four. We taped on and off from April 2019 to December 2019. My birthday in January 2020 made me thirty-five, and, as we all well know, still single. I am optimistic at the outset of the show. Here is a chance for me to work with a matchmaker, a.k.a. a pro and an expert in finding the ideal partner for someone, ready to help me find love. I resolve to openly express what I want in a future partner, as well as the inexorable conviction that I deserve such a partner. I am not just unapologetic to Sima on screen—I am unapologetic in life. I have watched my friends who are my peers and beloved to me all find wonderful and stable partners for themselves. I know luck hasn't been on my side, but I believe that is all changing, albeit a little later in life than anticipated. I feel I deserve someone as equally lovely as my friends' husbands, and I am certain I will find that person on this docuseries.

I quickly learn that's not true, as you already know too. But I can't help but still wonder about the true meaning (and purpose) of society's insistence that women be "flexible" and "compromising." Is it a tactic to keep us submissive? Is it an "easy" way to preserve the traditional societal family structure that has existed for hundreds of years? Is it complacency? An understanding that men do not feel the need to be flexible or compromise, because of their deep-rooted generational entitlement surrounding arranged marriages in South Asian culture? What is it that made this woman, Sima, insist that I was the one who had to do the work of compromising? That it was my mother who bore the responsibility of forcing me to comply with this structure of power? Why did she, from her small town of Gulbarga with her own arranged marriage at the age of nineteen, believe that it was only supposed to be this way—even now, thirty-some years later? I met Sima's husband and one of her daughters, as well as her assistant. They accompanied her to Houston when she came for that initial meeting with my family and me. Her husband was mild-mannered, very enthusiastic about showing me their pictures from their travels to Whistler, British Columbia, the week prior and appeared to be more than happy to play her sidekick on this adventure in TV world. So that led me to think she believes she deserves a spouse who supports her and treats her like a priority in their relationship. But she doesn't believe I deserve that? Interesting (or not).

To me it was also quite telling of her privilege, of being from a wealthy family that married her off in a favorable situation, as well as her general ineptitude in modern-day matchmaking. You see, Sima might be an OK matchmaker in her own Marwari community in Mumbai, one that subscribes to her traditional views surrounding caste, color, height, and power. But in the larger context of the world, the one outside her bubble, she is vastly ill-equipped to deal with modern-day matchmaking. Let me outline a few of my beliefs—and you can disagree with me, of course.

- A matchmaker should listen to her client
- A matchmaker should find a suitable match based on similar values between her client and the proposed suitor
- A matchmaker should not shove her own outdated beliefs on the family of her client

Again, just my own beliefs. But should I ever use a matchmaker again, I will be very clear about my beliefs. I am sure you would expect nothing less.

That is my takeaway from this whole experience. I've been asked frequently if I would ever use a matchmaker again, and since I am still looking for my partner, I would say yes. It is still an avenue that could potentially work and potentially introduce me to a wonderful guy. But when you're working with a match-maker, you're not only dating the men she brings to you. You are also in large part dating her. You have an awkward first date. You outline what you want out of the relationship. And you see if you mesh. Sima and I did not mesh. Outside the *Indian Matchmaking* show world, I would have never continued a relationship with her. But there we were, in my living room with a biodata in her hand. No other matchmaker for me to select. No other option for me to pursue. And honestly, no knowledge of what a match-maker relationship should even be like at that point. Only now, months after the show aired, am I able to reflect on a potential matchmaker's relationship to me and how, should I ever use one again, I will be much more upfront about my ideas surrounding the process and how it works best for me, the client.

Thankfully, years prior to taping the show, when my job was at its peak misery level, I decided to do what many millennials do—start a side hustle. Sure, my friends were getting married and having kids. But I knew what I loved, and I knew I had to try to funnel those interests into a business. On a long weekend trip to visit some family in London, I had drinks with a friend who went on Semester at Sea with me many years prior. We met at the Soho House in Notting Hill and sat wallowing about our day jobs to each other. Lindsay, my friend, asked about the business ideas I had shared with her on my last trip to London a few months prior. Those ideas had fizzled, but I knew something more concrete was bound to work. I wanted it to be about women traveling more, exploring the world, and feeling empowered to do so through a community. She was thrilled to brainstorm, and as we sat in that crowded room sipping on Moscow Mules from copper mugs, the concept came to light. We spotted celebrities and creatives at every table there, their presence egging us on to join their world of entrepreneurship and freedom from corporate jobs. *We could do this, maybe even together,* we posited as we kept ordering rounds of drinks.

Over the din of the room, we connected over our desire to share our knowledge of travel with others. What if we took women around the world with us? What if we took away all their excuses for why they could not travel? We could create our own dream itineraries, use our paid time off to lead the tours ourselves, and take care of everything from five-star accommodations to amazing cultural experiences, from cooking classes to incredible meals at the best restaurants in the areas. Trips would be one week long, so that no one had to be away from the office for more than that time. We would only stay at hotels that were of our own level of comfort. All that each woman signing up would have to do is book her own round-trip ticket and let us take care of the rest.

So many of our busy friends would be able to use our company as a resource for them to see the world. The study abroad we did, Semester at Sea, focused on locations that were not "typical." We would do the same. There are companies out there that do these group tours, but we would stand apart with our quality and attention to detail. We were sold on our own idea. We were both childless, though Lindsay was married to a wonderful guy. We were our own target demographic, and we believed we understood the market. While sometimes we felt "left behind" from the milestones our peers were reaching, we were both yearning for a life that included purpose through business and also one that included passion for our work. This was the answer.

We moved on quickly to discuss a company name. Something easy to say, slip into conversation, and type into Google. It hit me. In the United States, in offices around the country, coworkers give their peers black balloons on their fortieth birthday. A popular phrase plastered everywhere is "over the hill." I rebelled against that idea. There is nothing about forty that means your life is going downhill. In fact, I would argue that at that age your life is brimming with opportunity to truly experience the golden moments and to fully explore the world. Your thirties and forties are a time where you are more financially stable than ever and more established in your career to take a week off at a time to see a different part of the world. So no more of this "black balloon." This company would usher in every birthday with a golden balloon. A metaphorical celebration of the chances we have to live life on our terms. We loved it. And so, on New Year's Eve Eve (that's December 30) of 2018, this business was named My Golden Balloon. It was a shell with a name, and it was already loved dearly.

I went back to Houston a few days later, the hazy conversations about the company born from Moscow Mules on the forefront of my mind. I WhatsApped Lindsay and we set up a time to chat.

She had been thinking about our brainstorming session too. On our call, that first week of January 2019, we officially (with no drinks in front of us) went into business together, a 50/50 split of two friends separated by an ocean. Well, what does "business" look like? We decided we would start an Instagram account and I would post every day to build a like-minded community of women travelers. Lindsay would use her marketing, branding, and novice web design skills to start www.mygoldenballoon.com. The domain was purchased, the Squarespace account set up, and the Instagram account was linked to my personal account. We were off!

I would go to the office every morning, grab some hot tea, close my door, and sit down to create a post, often one showcasing a woman in a dreamy location with vibrant colors and an enticing caption about the locale. People started following us, each account a mini celebration as we organically grew through these daily posts. I would make sure to schedule calls only after 10:00 AM, and on days when I had depositions across town (or often across the state in which I was driving or flying), I would post at 6:00 AM. It was stressful to juggle tasks on the busy weekends or with the demands of my legal job, but I made it work. I started writing the content for the site with Lindsay's instruction. One week we needed the "About the Founders." The next week called for me drafting the Terms and Conditions and Privacy Policy. My legal skills finally had some real-world use. Progress was slow, tedious in fact. Trial prep on my end, deadlines on her end. A bout of the flu for me, an eye ulcer for her. Travels, travels, travels. After all, that was our life passion that started this whole endeavor. But we were in no rush and reassured each other that we would eventually "get there"—I believe "there" was the moment we made a single dollar.

I constantly followed our competitors, keeping tabs on their marketing campaigns, social media feeds, and news of venture capital funding. I wanted to know how this path we were traveling on might look one day. I was transitioning jobs in April 2019 and thought, *This is a great time to do some market research.* The company most similar to ours was offering a coed tour to Botswana for ten days. It was perfect. I would take a vacation, use the days wisely, and then put in my resignation and two weeks' notice. Just one hitch—the company representative I called after placing my order and getting a cancelation an hour later told me that only one spot was open on the trip. That one spot had to go to a guy, because the company assured each traveler they would be paired with someone of the same gender in the shared accommodations. I assured them I did not mind sharing a room with a male stranger. He was a fellow traveler, after all. I am sure we could respect each other's space. The representative told me they would not approach the traveler to even ask him because their priority was not putting him in an uncomfortable situation. Here I was, willing to pay over $5,000 for that last spot, and they were refusing on principle to even *see* if it could work. I was livid. The dates worked perfectly. The destination was ideal. And this company would not acquiesce. After venting to Lindsay on our weekly business meeting call, she pointed out the lesson in this experience. We too, as a company, would have to stick to our policies strictly from the outset. We too would have to say no to money in our pockets if it didn't fit into our mission or procedures. She was right. I knew it, but I still didn't like it. I called the company representative back asking for any other option in that time frame. "Argentina," she replied. I responded, "No, but is there anything else? Anything at all?" You see, Argentina never personally interested me. If I were to list every country I wanted to visit in the next five years (in an ideal world), Argentina would not even be on the list. But Argentina it was. So I sighed, paid the $4,200, and bought my own ticket, arriving in Buenos Aires and departing from Mendoza. The trip was only eight days away, so I quickly put the days off in my calendar, warded off the toxic partner who demanded I stayed in the office, and hit the road. (To be clear, I was going to hand in my notice the day I returned from the trip. This particular job environment was so negative and tumultuous that there was a strong chance I would just leave on the same day I gave notice. If you haven't worked in a large law firm, you might not understand this concept, but for me, this was the reality of the situation.)

I landed in Buenos Aires in the blink of an eye. The direct flight from Houston was a seamless, eight-hour overnight flight. While the trip was marketed as coed, the tour group included thirteen women and one man. He seemed more than a little surprised to be on this luxury tour with a gaggle of women, but he soon warmed up to this unusual situation, and us. A dashing Brit hailing from his expat posting in Hong Kong, he good-naturedly laughed when people would stop our tour group to ask if it was a taping of *The Bachelor*. We were unstoppable and quick friends, a crew of like-minded professionals who signed up solo for a trip to Buenos Aires, El Calafate, El Chalten, and Mendoza. Energies were high, and everyone was in vacation mode.

As malbecs flowed, stories were shared, and we discovered how similar we all were. The bubbliest woman was a recent widow. Only thirty-five, her inspiring love story brought tears to our eyes. She was healing through exploring the world and was so open with her love for her lost husband. Another woman woke up one day to her long-term, live-in boyfriend telling her he was leaving to go live in Bali. He was gone in a day, leaving their dream home under construction and their bonded families at a loss. She found out from a mutual friend that he was living out of his surf duffel bag, and she still couldn't quite fathom how the whole situation came about. She was beautiful, an empathetic teacher and an accomplished member of the British Army Reserve. Another woman opened up about the years prior to this trip, in which she watched her mother heroically battle cancer until she ultimately lost. Years of her life passed with only that focus on her family, and now she was ready to slowly begin putting herself first again. These stories were powerful. These stories were a reality to me. Not my own tale but ones that I could relate to, those that came with a surprise we could never have anticipated. Those that came with challenges, roadblocks, obstacles—and above all else, loss.

Many of these strong women were coming to terms, quite valiantly, with the fact that their lives were not on the strict timelines of their communities back home. They were not married yet. They did not have children yet. They were, by some standards, "behind" on hitting those life milestones. And without wallowing and with so much proactivity, these women rose up to the moment. They booked trips across the world to travel with strangers they had never met. They excelled in their careers. From teachers to high-level members of tech companies, to nurses and other health practitioners, they were at the top of their game. They were star aunts, loving daughters, and excellent friends to those they loved back home. These women left me in awe. In a strange twist of events, the Universe brought together these very people to show me that there was so much more to *living* than the milestones of marriage and children. And life can follow your very own timeline, that much I was now certain of.

What was interesting to me was the conversations with this group about timelines we can't control, the ever-underlying biological *ticktock* of a woman's body. I never liked that phrase, honestly. But as I grew older, sometimes I could actually feel the hum of time and its urgency if I wanted children. I have always been quite certain that I want a family. In fact, the two astrologers who have read my birth chart in the past assured me I would have sons. And more specifically, twins. Who knows? I'm not certain I subscribe to any absolute veracity of a star chart. But I always did know I at least wanted the family. And many of my new friends in Argentina felt the same way. Quite a few had frozen their eggs already, sharing harrowing stories of the process and the mental obstacles that are infrequently mentioned but always a part of the journey. They spoke of low egg count retrievals, the betrayal they felt by their bodies, and the instability caused by the hormonal changes at the core of the process. It sounded brutal, we all agreed—but many said it was on their 2019 to-do list regardless. They felt they had no choice but to ensure some sort of insurance policy for the families they desired. They reckoned they couldn't control the timing of meeting the right partner, but at least this gave them some semblance of control in creating their futures. I was pretty quiet as the conversations whirled around me.

I had gone to a reproductive endocrinologist when I was thirty, and again when I was thirty-three. He asked, "Why did you come to me? Everything going OK with conceiving naturally?" I stared at him blankly before explaining I was single, recently turned thirty, and didn't even have a boyfriend. This was just me checking. He cocked his head to the side. "Oh, OK. Good, good. Let's begin." He started with my "health history." I jumped straight to the age I got my first period. The doctor stopped me. "No, we will start at the beginning. Were you a preemie? Were you born premature?" I was stunned. That's the beginning of reproductive health? Yes, he assured me. That determines some of your reproductive health for sure. He's older, well renowned in Houston and likely the world. I waited four months to get my first appointment with him. I knew that would make me an existing patient of his for the next six to seven years according to medical recordkeeping. This was my own insurance policy. If and when I ever needed this doctor, as an existing patient, I could call and be seen earlier than a new patient could. We went through my history as he murmured *hmm, mhmm*s and asked question after question.

Next, we went into an examination room where I put on the gown and waited nervously. A female nurse came in with him, and they started the vaginal ultrasound. I gripped her hand tightly. I was not expecting . . . *that*. She laughed and petted my hand. The doctor was giddy within a minute. "My oh my, this is wonderful!" I smiled, relieved that the preliminary news was good. He asked if I wanted to see, and we stared at the ultrasound screen together. Looked . . . fine to me. To be clear, I had no idea what I was looking at, but he explained I appeared to be quite healthy. Blood work would be needed, but with my maternal family history of the women having babies into their mid-to-late forties, paired with this ultrasound, he felt we were moving in the right direction. The blood work results a few weeks later confirmed the same. I went back a few years later, three years to be exact, and all was well again.

So when the women in Argentina asked me point-blank if I would be freezing my eggs, I replied no. I was mindful of the risks, but I was comfortable with them for myself personally. And I was very well aware this was a personal choice. Mine would be to not freeze my eggs. I was going to play it by ear. I was going to believe with a certain pomp of optimism that the right partner for me would appear one day. And until then, I was going to enjoy the days, months, and years that I "waited" for him. I was going to pursue my side hustle with abandon, start leading tours for My Golden Balloon, and even make a move to New York City with no employment lined up and no idea how long I'd stay. The world was open for me. Oysters, and all the things, were mine.

So yes, I didn't get married at thirty, have my first child at thirty-two, or have that second child at thirty-four. But instead, I did so many amazing things that fulfilled me in ways I could have never imagined. From entrepreneurship, to world travels, to picking and moving to a brand-new city in my mid-thirties, I was the sole arbiter of my life. I was able to achieve anything—all the while knowing that even though my timeline might be different than my peers', it was my own. And the right guy, the one who knows Bolivia has salt flats, he's certainly just around the bend.

11

YOU'RE NOT A TREE. YOU CAN MOVE.

H ERE'S THE THING about everyone else living that "milestone-driven life," as I call it. If you don't run that same course, you're left to your own devices. Let me clarify: you are not "behind." But the practicality of it is, you are left on a less populated path. You won't be having the same dilemmas centering on *Do we move to the suburbs? Stick it out in town? Should our kids apply to pre-K programs in public schools? Is Montessori right for them? Would it be feasible to afford a bigger house soon?* That's not you. That's certainly not me.

At this age of thirty-six, when I thought I would be consumed by those family-centric adult decisions, I instead find myself making ones that leave me questioning *if* I'm an adult at all. I'm not just a late bloomer by many accounts. I'm a *late* late bloomer. Many of my peers spent a few years in New York in their early to mid-twenties. They reminisce over walk-up midtown East apartments shared with three girls. Drunken nights at Britney Spears concerts that ended with one-dollar pizza slices. The bottomless brunches that ruled their Sunday and left them struggling Monday at the office. And I never had those years. I had a version of it through visiting my friends there.

I had a version of it from living in Houston. But I also purposefully delayed all those early-twenties experiences, ranging
from financial hardship to reckless abandon, by going directly
to law school from university. I finished law school at the age
of twenty-five and started my first job with a six-figure income,
skipping entirely over those carefree ramen-eating New York
City days described fondly today by so many of my friends.

The COVID-19 pandemic was an interesting time that com-
pounded these feelings of "shoulda, woulda, coulda." As my
friends doubled down on family life and juggling work through
Zoom calls, I mainly dealt with the fallout from *Indian Matchmaking.* For a short period of time after the show came out in
July 2020, I tried a life where I worked full time and also did
press engagements and managed my social media. I rationalized that the period of chaos would be a short one—weeks if
not close to one month. By October, I was drained. Depleted.
Absolutely at my wits' end. The media's appetite for the show,
and by extension for me, was not slowing down. I was waking
up at 5:30 AM, responding to work emails, taking press interviews from 6:00 AM to 8:30 AM with Europe, working through
the morning with Zoom court hearings or frantic brief writing,
and finally making it to lunch where I would shovel food in
my mouth before doing American press. Afternoons were back
to work with interludes of any press that couldn't be squeezed
into the evenings or extended lunch breaks. Post-work would be
walking my dog Conan, eating a dinner unfit in its nutritional
content for a college student, and gearing up for 9:00 PM interviews with India and Asia. Those lasted until midnight before
I could curl up in my bed with my alarm set for the next day.
Ten weeks into this masochistic routine with its wellness fails,
I said goodbye to my legal job.

It wasn't an easy decision by any means. I poured over my financial statements and made Excel charts filled with hypothetical situations. I asked myself, *What do you need to live comfortably each month, paying all your bills and taking into account any incidental health, domestic, or auto situations that could require lump sums?* A monthly total appeared. I added $1,000 to that number so that I left some wiggle room. I evaluated my investments and further hypothesized how those might grow. I knew those would be my last line of defense. They could be liquidated slowly, selling off portions at a time if and when it ever came to needing those funds. The thought of ever touching my investment accounts rattled me, but I charged on with this evaluation. What about my savings account? Prior to Hurricane Harvey, it had been robust and thriving. It could have easily supported me for eighteen to twenty-four months. But losing your home and all your earthly possessions is, practically speaking, an expensive exercise. My savings account showed the monetary story of that disaster. Gone was the comfortable eighteen to twenty-four months of living expenses. Only six months was left. Why am I telling you all of this? Because I want you to know the behind the scenes of stepping away from a career path you've known for ten years. I want you to not look at social media accounts of those making these daring changes without also considering their assessments and forecasting. It's a really big deal, and from the outside, it looks like a rash decision to viewers. But for me, there was no choice left.

I knew I needed freedom. I needed a place to grow on my own terms. I need a place where my path wasn't so . . . solitary. A place where everyone hustled for a better tomorrow. A place where complacency was just simply not present. I was not a tree. I knew I could move. I needed to leave Houston. I needed to go to New York City.

Even before leaving my job in October 2020, I visited the city to see if I could imagine myself living there. I stayed with a friend and enjoyed another weekend of meeting up with friends, wandering the COVID-emptied city, including an eerie but serene trip to the Metropolitan Museum of Art and eating at all my favorite spots. I walked the Brooklyn Bridge, met up with a few of my castmates in person for the first time, and coordinated coffees and breakfasts with "Instagram friends"—my term for people who I had never met "IRL" but had communicated with extensively through DMs. I was floored by it all. These people, mostly women, were incredible. Whether they had children or not, partners or not, husbands or not, it didn't matter. They didn't speak of those details. They spoke about what they were building (businesses, media outlets, master's degrees, empires). They spoke about their travels. They spoke about what they wanted to accomplish this year, next year, in the next five years and beyond. This was my place. These were my people.

I planned to leave my job in October and move to NYC later that month. So, as you now know, the job did end in October. But then, because life can't be planned to a T, no matter how hard you try, the COVID numbers spiked around the country as news of a vaccine in early 2021 was announced. I made the executive decision to delay my move and take the time in Houston to recharge. I was exhausted. I had been running on adrenaline since July, and we were just now entering the start of holiday season, a.k.a. November. My holidays in Houston were a blur of slow days and lots of sleep. For the first time in my adult life, I was not working as an attorney. I started declining most press engagements. They still poured in, but I realized the toll of giving away those hours—the preciousness of my time. And what my time needed to be spent on was rest.

I was officially on sabbatical. I didn't need to check work emails. There was no need to appear for Zoom court hearings. There were no memorandums or briefs to review. There was no one to answer to but myself. I might not have moved to NYC *yet*, but these first vestiges of freedom were dear to me. Interestingly, when I announced my sabbatical, some of the first questions I was asked (and many that followed) centered around its end date and whether I was giving up the law forever. People wanted me to already know the end. I barely had figured out this beginning. I realized then it was their own personal tolerance for risk, and I understood quite acutely how risky this move was. I'll tell you one thing I learned about the legal field: firms and companies don't appreciate any time off on your résumé. Gaps on that one-page document indicate your lack of dedication. I understood I might not be able to return to law, or at least law as I knew it. And after nights tossing and turning to that realization, I came to terms with that fact. I took it was a sign from the Universe that this might be my "forced" conclusion to my legal career. I had been miserable for eleven years and counting. Was this the worst ending? Not at all. I gathered all my courage and told myself, *You'll make it. Somehow. Some way. You'll take care of yourself.* Many of my friends reassured me of the same. Many had left their careers and it worked out well, they shared. Well, yes. But I had to gently point out to each of these kind friends that they were able to follow their creative pursuits outside their formal career as a full-time gig because their partners were able to fully support their lifestyle. Many looked at me blankly before slowly nodding. "True," they said. "You're so right."

At my lowest moments in making this ultimate decision, I wished for a partner for an altogether practical function: a security net so that I could fly off into a new world of book writing and entrepreneurship with My Golden Balloon without worrying about liquidating my investments to survive. The feminist in me cringed at my own desire for a partner for this very "traditional" reason. But it was also practical, and I allowed those feelings to wash over me. They were feelings that life wasn't fair and *why can my friends do this so easily and for me it has to be so hard?* I had to come to terms with the fact that I had to do this alone. I had to plan my whole life around the prospect that I would potentially never have a partner. That included never finding a partner who would be my financial security net and also never finding someone who would be on my team, who would support my dreams, who would encourage me to take these leaps. My friends told me their husbands were their biggest cheerleaders for their dreams. They were, after all, a unit, and each of their dreams was thus a collective dream. Hearing this, I had honestly never felt lonelier. It wasn't just the money, let me make that clear. Ultimately, after all that soul searching, it was a lack of having my dreams supported by a unit that I was a part of. Sure, my family was behind me in their own right. Sure, my friends encouraged me along the way. But I understood that your partner could amplify your own strength to make these huge life moves, figuratively and literally.

The lesson I had to learn was clear. Of course I wanted a partner, but I had to learn how to live my life without any reliance on one. This was about independence. This was about belief in my own strength and capacity to survive. Nay, to thrive. I could do this alone. I knew it. And so the logistical plans began.

Step one: Get both doses of the COVID vaccine. Houston's systems in place made that easier than ever. Just weeks after it was made available to health care workers, my doctor informed me it was available to people like me who are immunocompromised. I was thrilled but also scared. With little to no vaccine safety data on those with autoimmune conditions, I was one of the people stepping up to take it first and to report on side effects and potential flare-ups. For me, it was an easy decision. I believe in the vaccine. I believe in science. So I took on the risk of the unknowns and hoped for a healthier tomorrow. I made the decision to share my story on social media and was so touched by those who connected with me to show their support. Many individuals with autoimmune conditions had questions for me and wanted to share in my journey, since their US cities were moving more slowly than Houston. Many outside the United States wanted to know how it played out with side effects the days after and beyond. This outpouring of connections made me realize how wonderful a social media platform *can* be. While it is sometimes used to spread hate, criticism, and falsehoods, it can also prove to be a space to share experiences, tell our stories, and join together in times of uncertainty.

Step two: Pick a date to leave. While I was fully vaccinated (both shots plus two weeks), I understood that a large number of New York City residents were not yet. I would wait for the cold weather to pass and for more vaccine access. April 1 became an arbitrary hard-and-fast date to leave for NYC. I would have enough time—five weeks—to scout out neighborhoods and pick an apartment with a June 1 lease start date. Five weeks seemed like a long stay, but I knew the days would pass by quickly. I wanted to enjoy the city too. I was still on sabbatical, and the thought of idle Tuesdays in the city sat quite well with me. They were aspirational, in fact. No business emails. Nowhere to be. The whole world would be busy working away, and in my mind, I would be alone to wander. That thought alone sounded positively decadent. Five weeks was set too.

Step three: Find a place to stay. This part proved to be challenging. From overpriced and dingy Airbnbs to websites connecting subletters to sublessors to even looking at five-week stays in hotels, I tried it all. I had my ticket booked for April 1, my mind set on five weeks, and nowhere to stay just ten days prior to leaving. It struck me, albeit quite delayed, to reach out to my extended network. My old friends in the area are settled in Brooklyn or now even Jersey with the families. No one had any insights into subletting for me. But after a quick reach out to an Instagram friend I had never met in person, I had someone on the search for me. By that evening, two of her friends contacted me and offered me their furnished places. I was floored by the kindness of this virtual stranger—*virtual* being both quite literal and figurative here. And I also quickly acknowledged to myself that "Aparna Not from *Indian Matchmaking*" would not have had this same opportunity to make this move seamless or just plain easier. This realization would hit me a lot over the course of my five-week trial run in the city. To be fair, the generosity of these people would always have existed it just would never have found its way to me. They would still be out there in the world helping anyone they happened upon—that's how wonderful they inherently are. But I would not have found them. I would not have had the pleasure of their assistance. I would not have had this home.

And the home was perfect. My friend's friend turned temporary landlord rented a sun-drenched studio on the top floor of a perfectly located West Village apartment building. He was living with his partner and his place was empty, so he left it sparsely furnished and emptied a closet and two drawers for me. I couldn't have asked for more. He met me when I arrived—tall, handsome, impeccably dressed in the most casual manner. I had explained to him in our brief texts and emails prior to my arrival that I was writing my book (this book!) and would be spending a lot of time in the apartment. I was not currently working but pursuing creative endeavors instead. He seemed fine with my brief description of my life in flux. When I met him, exhausted not only from the journey but also from the rushed days leading up to my trip, I felt I should explain to him a little more about my background. Standing there in sweats, an oversized drape sweater, and a ponytail, I told him about this "Netflix show" I was on last year, the sabbatical I took from my eleven-year career, and my intention to make my move to New York a full-time one. Yes, with no job, no significant other pulling me here, or a real plan even. He digested the information easily with a quick laugh. Disheveled and feeling wholly unimpressive, I asked, "What? You haven't been on a reality show?" He chuckled and responded that he had never been asked. Because in my world, reality show stars looked like this guy in front of me. They certainly didn't look like me. But here we were—he in his stable relationship with a stable job, probably seven to ten years my junior in age. Me with no relationship, no job, and a decade of experience that in that moment felt all for naught. It was laughable, even to me. Another refrain of my trial run started in that key exchange in the living room: *How did I get here?* I would ask myself that a lot in the next five weeks.

With a Home Depot copy of his key set, a quick tutorial of the TV remote (I didn't turn it on once the whole time I was there), and a show-and-tell with the air-conditioning unit, he was off and I was alone. I sat there on someone else's couch, in someone else's home, and saw my reflection in his floor-length mirror propped against the wall. I pulled out my phone and took one solitary picture. I bet right then that this moment would be the start of something great, perhaps even something enduring. The picture is one of a tired, triumphant, little lost, and a lot hopeful Aparna. I wondered even then, would this be something I smiled at fondly years from now? A lifetime into my New York living and so far down the road that I couldn't even imagine the macro, large-scale moments to come, such as: *Where would I live next? Who would I love later? What would I do for work down the road?* I had no idea. But I took the picture. Just for me, just in case.

The only plans I made off the bat were with a friend from my Argentina trip. Our favorite West Village spot, in a fitting turn of events, was now a short walk away. I turned on Google Maps, walked left from my street, and was immediately slapped in the face by gusts of wind. The temperature was in the low forties, and I was not prepared. I had forgone my overcoat in the packing selections, rationalizing that it would only be chilly for a few days before the city heated up. Side note: I stayed through early May. New York still has chilly days in May. But the naive Texan in me didn't know that when she packed for these five weeks. So there I was, huddled into a moto jacket with three layers on under it and fleece-lined leggings under my jeans. A short waddle down Seventh Avenue popped me straight to the friendly, heated, outdoor seating of the restaurant. I was relieved to see a friendly face on that chilly April night, and we settled right into plans on how I should tackle this period. I quickly tagged our delicious starters, the wine, and the candlelight in our little heated nook on Instagram before putting away my phone for a leisurely meal. We nibbled from dish to dish, filling up on all we could manage that night. Laughing together, we still ordered dessert to take a bite each. That's when we noticed the first group on the sidewalk pass us, turn, come back, and circle twice more. They were pointing at me and furiously tapping out texts. I was surprised anyone recognized me but just shrugged and moved on with my dinner. But then two young women passed our table, circled back, and poked each other violently, one loudly exclaiming, "I told you she tagged this restaurant."

I was stunned. My friend looked perplexed. "What was that about? Did you say you were here on social media?" I nodded yes. "Oof, you might want to rethink that moving going forward. Wait until you've left the place." I nodded again. It just hadn't been an issue in Houston—largely because I didn't go out in Houston. While the coronavirus infection numbers raged on in our southern city, I opted pre-vaccine to stay at home or, in rare instances, to meet for picnics with friends. In the short weeks since I had been fully vaccinated, I was too busy with family and prepping for the move to venture out much. Sure, I had a few fans stop me for a selfie or to say hi, but nothing like these groups here in NYC on night one. I rationalized that this was a fluke, most likely. The show had come out over eight months prior, and there were only going to be a few people who recognized me in this huge metropolis. I was sorely mistaken.

New York was definitely not Houston. I was stopped by gushing strangers when walking down the street (with a mask on) multiple times, almost daily in fact. I heard diners calling my name loudly as I strolled through busy restaurants' "dining areas" stretching out onto the street. I had no choice but to brace myself as I walked down the sidewalks through the open-air tables on my way home. I was asked for selfies in the middle of coffee shops. I recall a particularly harassed workday where I left the apartment to get a quick meal at a local coffee shop. Once there, I decided to work at one of the few indoor tables for a change of scene. After settling in, I started my admin tasks—the first being sending a wire transfer to my vendor contact in Kenya for a safari I was planning for My Golden Balloon. A feat in itself to travel to an African country in the middle of the pandemic, it was also proving difficult to wire large amounts of money to a bank account in Nairobi. Shocking, I know. I settled in to google which of my two banks would be easiest to work with, searching for

PDF instructions that might demystify why my money was not being transferred. Panicking with deadlines of payment coming up, I also sat on hold waiting for a bank representative to answer my never-ending questions on failed transfers. After an hour of getting nowhere with this all-important to-do list task, a woman stopped en route to her own table. She poked her friends, whispered loudly that it was "Aparna from that *Indian Matchmaker* show," and proceeded to approach me while I sat on the phone. The representative came on the phone at that very moment. Trying to juggle explaining my need to send tens of thousands of dollars to Kenya while these well-meaning fans surrounded my table, gushing and asking for life updates, was absolutely overwhelming. I was reminded in that very moment that my fledgling travel business that was hardly off the ground was not going to take the driver's seat. Not in that moment anyway, and not at many other points where this post-show reality was going to creep in and navigate my life vehicle, whether I instructed it to or not. The loss of control and the loss of anonymity were not lost on me as I asked the bank representative on the other end of my cell phone to wait a moment, so I could take a selfie with these three women. The bubbly group invited me to dinner with them the next week. I politely told them I was busy. They pointed out they hadn't told me which day. I explained that every night was packed, since my visit was so short.

I was being honest. Every day and night was endlessly busy. I learned after the first week that I had to schedule only two meals or meetups a day, because otherwise nothing else was accomplished—with my business or my book writing or my social media sponsorships. I enjoyed every outing. I was getting to explore the city and explore new friendships, all at once. There were birds and stones in some analogy, but I was too rushed to even do the simple math on that scenario. My DMs were filled with incredible women I had already connected with prior to my trial run in New York City, and they were happy to have me in their hometown. And I was equally happy to be there. I lived day-to-day life one beautiful spring verb at a time. I "caféd." I strolled. I exhaled. I sat on warm stoops in the West Village en route home—because I could. I put headphones in and listened to my favorite old tunes. I took my headphones out and honed in on the sounds of the birds chirping coupled with cars bumping down the tiny neighborhood roads, too narrow for vehicles in both directions but somehow large enough for the occasional construction truck or street cleaning truck, their noise deafening for short moments. It was all welcome to me.

These women would be my most monumental friend first dates. I would be carefully evaluating our vibes and if we fit as real friends or if we would relegate one another to occasional acquaintance. Because, candidly speaking, I already missed my own friends. A lot. As the weather slowly warmed up in post–COVID vaccine New York, picnics were springing up every-where. Friend groups, large and small, gathered along the water on grassy patches or on relegated lawns at Washington Square Park, which I would invariably walk through each weekend. I would slow down my gait to watch people laughing loudly, clink-ing their plastic glasses filled with sparkling wines, petting their pandemic puppies, and knowing that they belonged to that group of people around them. That belonging was so easy for them. The way it would be so easy for me with my own friends if they were all living in this urban utopia. We would sit on blankets without a care about the world around us and only wrapped up in each others' jokes, gossips, and passing commentary on life goings-on. We wouldn't notice the lonely Indian girl watching us from the corner of her eye as she passed us. Those people picnicking certainly didn't notice me. So I had to make friends and hope one day I too would have a Manhattan group to call my own.

That started with these coffees and dinners, these brunches and matchas, these al fresco lunches and late evening cocktails. And I was wowed by the people I got to know. These women were tenacious, spunky, full of grit and wisdom—all at once. There was a stronger potential for long-term friendship with some compared to others. I'll admit that here. I still remember how touched I was when one of them texted me after a breakfast "date." She hoped to see me again and told me, "You feel like an old friend." I was bowled over, floored by this frank and candid admission from this amazing woman. I admired her so much and was glad she appreciated my company as well. Overall, I loved them all.

I also knew that I would have never met these incredible individuals in that alternate universe that always exists in my mind nowadays—the one in which I never went on *Indian Matchmaking*, the one in which no one knew my name, the one in which this move would have been so incredibly different and so much lonelier. I would have potentially still moved to New York City. But in that other reality, I would be so alone. I reason that I would have done what many others do when they move to a new city in their thirties. They join book clubs and affinity groups and meet friends of friends, slowly growing their own cohort. There is a Facebook group called Little Brown Diaries that I used to love being a part of when it started years ago. It was a nationwide group for South Asian women to share their collective experiences, to ask for help or advice, to find wedding vendors and new jobs. It was brilliant. I speak in the past tense not because the group is no longer in existence but because I saw its ugliest side post–*Indian Matchmaking*. Initially, there was a post that the show was coming out. Someone saw the trailer and exclaimed that virtual watch parties should commence on launch day, July 16. Nadia, whom I had never met before but who I knew was a participant in the show as of a day prior to this post, tagged me in it. A shared laugh for us—two strangers in the world connected by this show that had excited this Facebook group of thousands of South Asian women. I suspected at that point these might be the only viewers of our show. I commented back to Nadia with a smiley face. It took a few days to turn that excitement to the polarized messages of love and vitriol. This group *hated* me. They unabashedly despised me, many knowing full well I was a member of their group. The comments were in the hundreds, if not thousands. Nadia was a princess, a queen, a victim of horrible men. I was a bitch, an ogre to the men who were subjected to dates with me, an elitist shrew. And to top it off, their vitriol was not only relegated to me but to my mother as well. I no longer saw the merit of this group that tore down women in their own community for their portrayal on an edited television show. I no longer trusted this warm, fuzzy community who could so easily turn on their own. Who were these trolls? Where was their sisterhood? Where was their decency? Lost apparently, somewhere in the cyber sphere. And I was hurt, betrayed, and disappointed.

As you might recall, I came up with a rule of confirming friend requests on Facebook if someone had mutual friends with me. Somewhere along the way, I confirmed a woman I had never met who had many of the same acquaintances as me. When she saw me move to New York City, she added me to the Little Brown Diaries New York chapter. I almost declined but then thought, *No, Aparna. They might tell each other which doctors to go to, which dry cleaners can properly clean saris or expensive lehengas, which grocery store carries an ingredient you might need.* It was a worthwhile group to passively join, never asking a question but consuming tips as needed. Once I accepted the invitation into the group, I did see some helpful insights right off the bat. I was pleased and jotted down the name of the best chai in town and the acupuncture spot most recommended in downtown Manhattan. And then I saw a post from a woman who had moved to the city on the same day as me. She was new in town, she explained. She would love to meet up with others, new and old to the city. The response was overwhelming. So many women responded to her, and a WhatsApp group was started for a large group meeting on a rooftop. I wanted to join them. "Alternate Universe Aparna" wanted to be included in that group. "This Universe Aparna" knew it wasn't possible. It was too much of a gamble. What if this was a group of women who agreed with those horrible comments from ten months prior? What if they had written them? What if I ruined their whole gathering my showing up that day? It was best that I relegated myself to the women who reached out to me, the real me. I knew I was lucky to have the outpouring of interest in getting to know me, but I also missed days when no one wanted to know me. It made no sense, rationally, but I found myself tearing up anyway. Sitting alone in my apartment, I closed the group post and put down my phone.

I was on my own here.

But I was not always lonely. Sometimes I was just alone. And there is a huge distinction. Lonely is when you need someone. Alone is when you are figuratively with no one else, physically by yourself. When I would wander the city by myself, I was most often content. Or even better than content, I was in wonderment that I was there. I couldn't believe I had done it finally, that these streets were my home. My roots were deep in Houston, but I was replanting myself in this urban jungle. I was proud of myself. But I didn't enjoy what others called "my fame." I don't like that word to start off. It still makes me uncomfortable. And I had never been so acutely aware of those who chase it or are just even enamored by it than I was in New York. I've never been one to be starstruck by a "proper" celebrity. I've dined next to Tom Hanks's table and had drinks next to Jennifer Aniston and her friends. I passed Nicole Kidman and Taylor Swift in Nashville all the time when I went to law school there. I never once said hello, ogled them, or snuck a picture. Not even when Taylor Swift was canoodling with John Mayer at a local restaurant at the height of their relationship. (Imagine my restraint! Or more likely my inherent disinterest.) I let them live their lives, knowing I had only a right to consume them through a screen. But that seems lost in today's world. And I only know it because of the insistence from some of my own fans to take pictures with me, force themselves into private conversations, and yes, even interrupt my dates. I am not a professional actor, and when these people saw me on their screens, they saw my home, my family, and yes, even my first dates. So it seems this gives many of them the idea that they now have access to me when I am dining out, walking down the street, or sitting on the subway.

It's a particular phenomenon I had only heard about from Shekar, who lived the "fame" in its post-show fervor in Chicago. I had briefly experienced it whenever I left Houston prior to the trial run, like on a trip with friends to Utah or even when I was in Chicago in business and saw Shekar for a few dinners. But the sustained experience of it over five weeks was frankly difficult. It wasn't the friendly visitors to my table or those who approached me with nice compliments. Those people were overall quite sweet and appreciative of the fact that I was giving them my time. I made it a point to introduce anyone who came up to me to everyone in my company, so that they were even more acutely aware that I was with friends (or family or a date) and chose to also respect that person's time and privacy. It usually worked. The instances that irked me were when I'd be putting a bite of food in my mouth and I'd look up to see someone pointing their phone's camera at me. Or when I was sitting on the subway and would peripherally see someone taking a picture of me. Never asking permission, just accessing me—at my best or my worst—because they felt a right or a need to do so. It was baffling. It remains perplexing today and likely always will to me.

Being a contributor to the first season of a show is a particular phenomenon—one in which you never knowingly signed up for whatever was coming in the months or years following the show airing on global television. Here's the thing: I needed time to accept it. And I needed more time to grieve a life of anonymity. It turns out I'm a relatively private person on a day-to-day basis, or at least aspire to be. Sure, I signed up for a show where cameras followed me around for maybe fourteen days total. I was OK with it. I enjoyed it as a unique experience. However, I did not know that the entrance of those cameras would put me bang smack in a situation two years later where I avoided eating with chopsticks for fear of missing my mouth, which for me is quite normal with my poor dexterity. After all, someone would catch that on their phone and post it goodness-knows-where. I did not know those cameras would mean I would have to take selfies in the middle of department stores, coffee shops, museums, and parks a lifetime later. I did not know any of it.

I wouldn't change the experience of participating in the show at all, mind you. But I would have prepped myself better. After a full-on COVID lockdown in Houston, a large part of this shock was just being out in public every day again. Coupled with the sharp increase in human interaction and a sudden (and ongoing) run-in with this alleged fame, I was in for a growth journey of epic proportions. I'd most closely compare it to the five stages of grief: denial, anger, bargaining, depression, acceptance. I was, after all, grieving the alternate universe that diverged further and further from its departure point with my actual reality. Some would say I was ungrateful. Heck, sometimes I even accused myself of the same when I was most irked or tired or defeated. But that's oversimplifying it. Maybe I did wish it would all go away . . . *sometimes*. But other times, I was overly joyous for everything this newfound notoriety afforded me. Friendships with like-minded women. Opportunities to find a gorgeous sublet in the city through my network. A book deal in which I was given the greatest gift to tell my own story. A flexible schedule while on sabbatical from my legal career to soak in these special days in the city. And of course, endless chances to live life on my own terms, the most special treasure of all in this Universe I now lived in. I just had to get to a place where I lived only in that last phase of acceptance. The trial run for five weeks in NYC was a toe-dip opportunity to see where I needed to regroup, re-collect, and revive when I returned to Houston before making my permanent move to Manhattan later that summer.

Acceptance took a little longer than my time spent in the city. It followed me home to Houston, knocking on the door and wanting to be let in once and for all. I landed on a Friday night and went straight to my best friend's child's first birthday party the next day. The celebration was at 9:30 AM on an already humid May day. My old friend group milled about, their children in the playground, their attention half on the little ones and half on catching up with another. News was shared with me—it was string of announcements that so-and-so was moving to the suburbs. The kids were all about to turn four or five, and the schools were just better out there. They were right, and it was easy for me to congratulate them.

I already knew I didn't need them to stick around Houston's city limits to hang out with me. I'd be long gone in no time. I was replanting myself, after all. As I studied them one by one, those friendly faces suddenly looked foreign to me. I wondered if any of them would be at my child's first birthday party one day. Likely not. Not even my two best friends. I'd likely live across the country and be far from this world. They could hypothetically fly in for it, but that doesn't even make sense rationally. It's just a child's first birthday—a sweet smash cake and a few friends to make the event jolly. Nothing to travel across the country for. I wondered who *would* be there? Nameless faces of people I had yet to meet? Or maybe some of the faces I had been blessed with meeting this past month? I didn't know. What I did know is that they were going further down the milestone-marked path, and I had already turned off it, firmly making direct aim for another future altogether. I was sad. But I was also angry. That's the thing with those five stages of grief. They aren't simple. Grief isn't linear. You can make it to the last step of acceptance and find yourself back at denial in one fell swoop. You might make a visit to anger along the way to acceptance, perhaps. Or maybe you sit awhile at bargaining. It's all possible in your steps of grief.

I was surprised to feel anger, though. That's not a common feeling for me. I usually skip right past anger and sit with hurt and betrayal. But for some reason, I couldn't shake the anger that my life *had* to be so different when I just wanted the same things as my friends in Houston. A wonderful partner, a family of my own, and a house with a literal white picket fence. If someone had asked me my dream for myself ten years ago or one year ago, it was always the same—it was always the utopia I just described. That was as big as my dreams ever got. They never stretched to any sort of fame or fortune, only to a steady and stable life filled with the beauty of mundane routine. And yes, I looked around at the flux I was living in at age thirty-six, and it was something I had never imagined for myself. But then, a miraculous thing happened. When I sat with the anger and let it pass through me, I also realized that as it turns out, the world was going to be bigger for me. Whether I liked it or not, I was not going to have an ordinary life. The Universe had bigger plans for me than I had for myself, and I had to be OK with it. Thrilled would come later when I could see the results. But while I lived through the uncertainty and not knowing, I had to know that this was all a part of my unique life path. And so acceptance came; it washed over me in a *whoosh*. The same *whoosh* in which we fall in love—and out of love. I fell into acceptance for a future I did not yet see or understand.

And I was at peace with it. In fact, it made me even more aware that I had to push further. I had to go down a path that included not only finding new friends in a new city but also finding a life partner. That starts with finding someone you'd like to date, the someone who turns into your boyfriend. And for that, I knew I would need to muster the courage to get back on the dating apps. So, in true Aparna fashion, I got on four of them in one night. I reactivated accounts that had been dormant for over a year. I revised the bio section, threw up a few new pictures, and voila! I was back in the dating scene—but this time in New York City. In between working on this book's first-draft deadline, seeing my few old friends in the area, going on friend dates with women I had only "met" on Instagram, and looking for an apartment, I must admit, not much time was devoted to dating on this trial run. I did go out with a man from the apps. He was in finance, made reservations at an impressive craft cocktail bar (maybe the actual reservation-making was the impressive part), and we had a few drinks together on a rainy night. I had a nice enough time chatting with him and made a note that I should say yes to a second date. Midway through our date, a fan came up to the table for a selfie. His face scrounged up momentarily. The server laughed when she left, adding that she too was a fan. I was so flattered. A glance again to my date. His eyes were narrowed. Toward the end, after he had happily ordered his second drink, he explained that he was in private equity and working hard toward taking his boss's job when he left next year. He was a little surprised to see how "public" my life was and could not imagine that for himself. It didn't quite hit me in that moment that he was politely telling me, *your life is too much for me to take on.* He said it so casually, so conversationally. But after he paid the check and hopped in his Uber, he paused to say goodbye again. "Good luck with everything. I'm looking forward to reading your book one day." And he was gone. I was planning on walking home, so I turned on my heel and left hurriedly as the drizzle turned into full-on raindrops. I was shocked. Did this guy just effectively give me the "all the best," a.k.a. never going to see you again, goodbye? It appeared he did. And it appeared it was because of my alleged stardom. Hmm, this was a new twist to dating post–*Indian Matchmaking.*

Another date was a sweet guy who slid into my DMs. I was always against that method of meeting someone, but when he messaged me, he seemed so normal. We had a mutual friend. His Instagram profile showed pictures of him traveling and with his niece. We had one mutual friend, who was someone I respected fully. It was promising. My friends asked me to drop my pin, since he was a technical "rando." And our date was . . . nice. We didn't have too much in common, but I appreciated the normalcy of it all. I appreciated him. I declined our second meetup the next evening but at least felt there was promise to meet someone on the same page as me in this city.

I am admittedly terrible at staying consistent with logging on to these apps, which I think many millennials can attest is one of their issues with using them as well. Often, days (even weeks) will pass by before I log back in to see a string of messages from matches. In my haste to join multiple apps, I joined one for South Asians and matched immediately with a handful of men. In an attempt to be proactive, I messaged them all, asking them how their weekend was going. I hopped off, feeling like I had conquered the world with these small, seemingly insignificant actions and headed out to meet my cousin for drinks by the water. While we chatted away as the sun set over the water and the far-off Statue of Liberty, a friend of mine entered the bar with her boyfriend. She was there for a birthday party and invited me to join them on the roof once I wrapped up with my family. I agreed, eager to meet others in the city who were around my age too. When I arrived at the large private party, I felt immediately awkward as eyes glanced over to assess me. I asked my friend who the birthday guy was so that I could start by thanking him for letting me crash his party. She pointed him out across the bar. I sauntered up to him, trying to appear casual and friendly. When he saw me, he looked startled, if not momentarily stunned. I chalked it up to being "Aparna from *Indian Matchmaking*," wished him a happy birthday, and offered to buy him a drink, since I had, after all, invited myself to join his celebration. He was kind and extended a warm welcome and big smile. I didn't speak to him much, took a quick picture with him and a few of our friends before leaving, and didn't think anything of the encounter. A few weeks later, I logged back on to the South Asian–focused app. I had a message. It was the birthday boy from the rooftop party. He thanked me for coming and said he hoped I had fun. My mortification quickly turned into laughter. Of course I would match with a guy, message him with a quick question about his weekend plans, and then show up to his birthday party less than two hours later. It was comical and a good reminder that this seemingly huge city was in actuality a tiny town—one I was looking forward to knowing more about each day. While my first foray into dating didn't go swimmingly, I had great hopes for what was to come. Adventure awaited me here in this new home of mine. And I was so glad I had taken a chance and brought myself into this world that was truly meant for me. The future was certainly bright.